Conference room, Reinhold Publishing Corporation, New York.

NEW HORIZONS

IN

COLOR

by Faber Birren

Reinhold Publishing Corporation New York

Copyright 1955

Fourth Printing, 1960

Reinhold Publishing Corporation

Library of Congress Card No. 55-6281

Printed in the United States of America

Contents

Color Plates and Charts

To

LaVerne Bovee

friend and associate over many years

Preface

Although not trained as an architect, I have had an active interest in architectural color problems for well over twenty-five years. During this time I have gathered notes for this present book, undertaken a bit of scholarly study in history and tradition, worked hand-in-hand with architects and decorators, and attempted to shape new principles out of many contacts in the fields of industrial production, illumination, ophthalmology, and psychiatry.

On the more theoretical side I have studied the elusive properties of color harmony and human emotion, striving to find new relationships between color and form, between the physical reality of color and the strange reactions that seem to arise from it. Using the term *psychodécor,* I have tried a rather new approach which may one day lead to a more potent use of color in the field of architectural design and decoration.

On the practical side, I have written color plans and specifications for industrial plants, office buildings, hospitals, schools, stores, and commercial establishments. The research done and the results gained will be found reviewed in several chapters of this book and will perhaps be of the greatest value to the reader.

However, my preferred interest is in the realm of human vision, emotion, and psychology. If there has been anything unique in my endeavor, it has centered around an attempt to find new values for color to aid human efficiency and well-being, to contribute to human comfort and to control human moods. I am convinced that the old process of color selection based on such vague things as good taste and personal feeling will one day give way to a more penetrating knowledge of the human psyche and of the factors in color that seem to influence it.

I have tried to make this book both useful and provocative. Architecture and decoration are vital forces. And color which in the past has been more or less coddled for its esthetic and pleasurable qualities should be better understood and applied. Surely it can be made far more of a dynamic and essential force in modern life.

FABER BIRREN

New York, 1955

Fundamentals of Color Conditioning

Some years ago the selection of color in architecture and decoration was largely a matter of "good taste." The attitude was an artistic one, with the color scheme bold or conservative, depending on the emotional propensities of the creator.

To some extent this situation has not changed. Home interiors and exteriors still have good reason to express the personality of those responsible for them as designers or owners. Individuality in a hotel lobby, a cocktail lounge, an exclusive shop may effectively and profitably follow the creative viewpoint.

Yet as architecture in the last twenty years has become more functional and less ornate, so has the selection and use of color in many types of buildings become more utilitarian. The emphasis has gone from appearance to purpose.

A Special Field of Expression

As technical advancements make building more and more complex, the architect and the decorator find themselves increasingly dependent on trained authorities in such fields as acoustics, air conditioning, illumination — and now color. This specialization requires some measure of scientific background and research method. Color coordination when capably handled cannot help but be practical. Whereas much engineering work concerns things that are definitely behind the scenes, color is a medium that is very much in prominence and therefore very important insofar as human impressions are concerned. The designer who does a good job of color is sure to find his efforts commended, for color is integral with design and form.

Why Functional Color?

To dip briefly into history, the use of color in architecture and decoration was once symbolic. Before the Renaissance an elaborate ritualism was followed that had to do with religion, astrology, mythology, the planets, the points of the compass, and other such involvements. Spiritual and emotional qualities for color came later in the Renaissance of the fourteenth and fifteenth centuries. It was not until then that things abstruse were pursued and the artist was freed to convey his "feelings" without reference to symbolic conventions and traditions.

Today, however, a new *functionalism* for color has come into existence. Like the symbolism of olden times it is less concerned with individual feeling than with a search for broader and more social values having to do not only with man's pleasure but also with his efficiency, comfort, and well-being. The old attitude of letting one man's personality dominate color choice is being replaced (and perhaps rightfully so) by an objective study of the human needs and desires of all men.

A home owner may insist that his fancies be indulged. Yet the indulging of fancies will hardly do for:

A factory owner who wants to lower accident frequencies and better the production of his workers.

Hospital trustees concerned with psychotherapy and aids to convalescence.

School boards concerned with child welfare and child health.

An office manager who wants to improve the efficiency and morale of his staff.

A store owner who wants to sell merchandise by appealing to the taste of his customers.

A hotel keeper who wants to have his suites satisfy his guests rather than himself.

Mayors and town-planning commissioners wishing to have the public favor municipal projects rather than complain about extravagance in high office.

Such problems are not, of course, to be solved very well through guesswork, insight, or individual persuasion.

Where color may be judged esthetically, one man's opinion is perhaps as good as another's. As in the art of painting, the virtues of one school of beauty over another have no criteria other than arbitrary prejudices or preferences. With functional color, however, this is not altogether true. Functional color may be defined as a system or method of color application in which definite objectives are set up and in which results are determined by measurement. In other words, beauty is made subservient to utility, and pleasure becomes a by-product of purpose.

The Beginnings of Research

Color conditioning (functional color) had its beginnings about three decades ago. During the early and mid-twenties the lighting profession had succeeded in attaining high levels of artificial light in the hospital surgery which obviated the need for daylight sources. With greater illumination, glare factors became next to intolerable and the white operating room of the past was destined for change.

At that time studies by ophthalmologists and surgeons led to the development of softer shades of green and blue-green. These colors reduced glare and complemented the red tint of human blood and tissue. For once, function rather than appearance was the chief consideration.

Subsequently, similar research was conducted in schools. The first industries to apply the benefits of color conditioning were in the pharmaceutical field, where the medical aspects of color could be understood. Difficult problems in the filling of phials and the threading of surgical needles were well surmounted with proper light and proper control of background.

Scientific Objectives

The objectives of color conditioning in factories, schools, hospitals, and offices are:

Improved production.
Better workmanship.
Fewer seconds and rejects.
Relief from eyestrain and fatigue.
Fewer accident hazards.
Shorter periods of worker-training.
Finer morale and lower rates of absenteeism and labor turnover.
Higher standards of plant housekeeping and care of equipment.
Better public and industrial relations.

It goes without saying that everything seen by the human eye is colored. Although illumination is an important factor, it has meaning solely in terms of the objects and surfaces that reflect it.

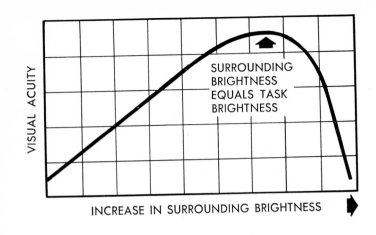

VISUAL ACUITY

SURROUNDING
BRIGHTNESS
EQUALS TASK
BRIGHTNESS

INCREASE IN SURROUNDING BRIGHTNESS

Effect of surrounding brightness on visual acuity, with the brightness of the task held constant. Seeing improves until surrounding brightness equals task brightness. Beyond this point, glare may handicap vision. After Lythgoe.

Brightness Engineering

Illumination is but one factor in designing an efficient and comfortable environment. As Luckiesh has stated, "A visual task is inseparable from its environment . . . High visibility, ease of seeing and good seeing conditions are overwhelmingly the result of good brightness engineering."

Although sharp contrast assures high visibility, visual comfort and efficiency may be better served with moderate brightness differences, particularly in concentrated tasks. Here the gray background might be superior to the black for prolonged effort.

The effect of surrounding brightness on visual acuity has been well explained by R. J. Lythgoe of England. If the illumination on a task is kept constant, and the surrounding brightness raised, visual acuity will improve. This improvement will be gradual and constant *and will be at its maximum when the surrounding brightness is slightly lower than, or equal to, the task.* Where the surrounding brightness greatly exceeds that of the task brightness there will be a rapid falling off in performance. As one ophthalmologist concludes: "Under certain conditions . . . extreme contrasts are desirable, as when an object near the threshold of acuity must be made visible, but, in

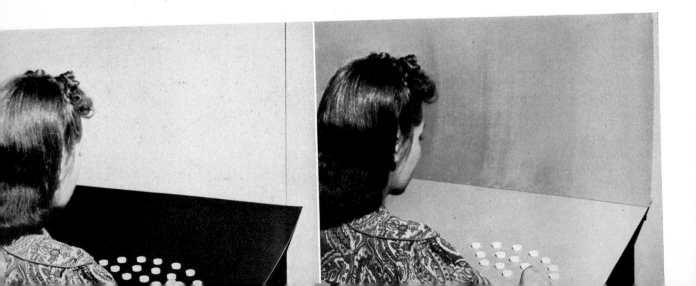

general, pronounced and useless differences in brightness in the field of vision contribute to ocular inefficiency and the production of fatigue. This is especially true when the eye in its movements must subject the central portion of the retina to frequent and sudden changes in intensity of stimulus. The inability of central vision to meet these demands for repeated rapid adjustment results in temporary partial blindness — central scotoma. For greatest comfort the entire field of vision should be well and evenly illuminated, with perhaps a mild increase in the area of the working plane" (Le Grand H. Hardy).

Brightness Ratios

The lighting profession has given tremendous emphasis to the need for low brightness ratios. It is said that the ratio of surrounding brightness to task brightness should be unity for best results. Ratios of from 10 to 1 to the more preferable 3 to 1 are, however, all satisfactory and approved. (Brightness ratios are determined as follows: assuming an even distribution of light, an area of white, for example, may reflect 85 per cent and black 3 per cent. Here the ratio would be over 28 to 1.)

Low brightness ratios, however, are no panacea. An all-white room might have uniformity and yet be intolerable. As a rule, the wall color should not greatly exceed the lightness of human skin (about 50 per cent), otherwise a person's appearance may suffer, the pupil of the eye may be unduly constricted, and most things seen may be blurred. Soft colors are not to be feared, despite the contrary opinions of some lighting experts.

View of a Softone desk, finished in an industry-wide standard of the Wood Office Furniture Institute. This special smoky gray, developed with the assistance of Faber Birren, has an ideal reflectance to "cushion" visual shock between the bright and dark areas common to the decoration of many offices. (James R. Dunlop photograph.)

Illumination vs. Color

In the author's opinion, illumination is too often given an unwarranted amount of importance in interior design. Lighting systems devised to triple or quadruple the volume of illumination may often defeat their own purpose, introduce glare, lead to complaints and actually lower human efficiency and production. An eye specialist has good reason to be skeptical about "rules" which establish definite levels of footcandles for certain tasks. Unless the environment is rightly controlled as to brightness and color, it is impossible to achieve the ideal balance.

It probably is safe to generalize that uniform brightness in the field of view is tolerable where ratios do not exceed 10 to 1, but where the use of white is not excessive. The task itself, however, may be 'black on white if it is relatively small in area. What must be avoided are severe contrasts in the major field of view (generally about 60 degrees surrounding the task — or 360 degrees if the worker constantly moves or looks about).

In the average industrial plant, office, or school the occupant works on dark materials such as metal, black office machines, black type on white paper — seeing these areas against dark tables, desks, and floors. If the building is old, there may be 10 footcandles or less of illumination — hardly enough to see clearly.

A new lighting system may be installed, possibly to deliver 25, 50, or more footcandles. And to effect the most impressive light-meter readings, the walls may be painted white. The higher level of illumination will no doubt be welcome, but the white walls may promptly cause trouble.

It is not difficult to analyze the errors that might be made. If the white walls are showered with illumination, brightness ratios (in relation to materials, machines and floors) may jump way beyond 100 to 1. Various things may happen. The pupil of the eye may be constricted to reduce visibility of dark materials and machines. Vision may be blurred and real distress noted. Pupillary adjustments to the brightness of the wall (which is unimportant) will be accomplished in a matter of seconds. The dark materials and machines (which *are* important) will not be so easily fixated — the reverse action of adjusting (from light to dark) being slow and time-consuming. The bodily reflexes of the individual may therefore be retarded and his productive capacity cut down. And all despite more light and brighter surroundings.

It would be wrong, of course, to argue against higher levels of illumination. However, if they necessitate glare and excessive brightness ratios, then it would be better to sacrifice a few extra footcandles for a more uniform and comfortable seeing condition. However, other devices may be brought into play to effect good illumination as well as good seeing.

In the situation described above, the glare of white walls could be offset if other areas and surfaces in the interior were also lifted in brightness. If the floor were concrete, for example, it could be scrubbed and bleached out with a caustic solution. Wood floors could be cleaned, or new floors in light materials might be installed. Machinery and equipment, desks and tables, could be painted lighter. This would be "lifting" the matter of brightness from the bottom up — an excellent and recommended practice. Yet if the floor were wood block, oily and dark, the machinery color and the wall colors would have to be kept on the subdued side.

Those who think in terms of illuminating efficiency are always campaigning for white and off-white colors on walls. Those who understand human vision and the psychological aspects of seeing are inclined to favor fairly soft hues. And in the author's experience, greater justification would follow this latter viewpoint. Practically all experimental evidence has shown that a surrounding field *darker* than the brightness of the task is far superior to lighter surroundings! The lighter surroundings will, in truth, tend to constrict the pupil and very seriously compete for attention. Thus it is safer to be on the moderate side than on the light side in almost any application of color.

2

Dynamics of Seeing

Vision is a remarkable sense, involving a number of fascinating phenomena. Only in recent years, however, has its magic been adequately studied and analyzed. Use of the eye and mind may consume as much as 25 per cent of the energy of the body. Good health is essential to good vision and good vision to proper health. For when the eyes are abused, the whole organism may undergo an adverse reaction. Diet will affect vision, as will disease, illness, and even mental condition. As science contends, the eye is really an outgrowth of the brain and not merely an attached organ.

Thus the control of the environment through illumination and color becomes an important art that may well contribute to human welfare.

Vitamin Deficiency

Vitamin A deficiency adversely affects vision. During World War II important contributions were made to human efficiency — and human vision — through the encouragement of proper dietary habits in industrial plants making war materials. Where there is deficiency of vitamin B_1 (thiamine), diseases such as beri-beri are found, in which there is severe dilation of the pupil of the eye, poor vision, and general debility. In vitamin B_2 (riboflavin) deficiency the skin may grow rough, red, and cracked. This vitamin is readily destroyed by ultraviolet. Vitamin C deficiency produces scurvy and extreme redness of the eyes. Vitamin D deficiency, like that of vitamin A, is related to night blindness and may produce opacity of the lens.

Interior of house designed
by John G. York, architect.
Courtesy of *Progressive
Architecture.*

The Effect of Disease

In a previous book by the author, *Color Psychology and Color Therapy,* considerable space has been devoted to the effects of disease upon the human eye. Simple ailments such as influenza or abscessed teeth may cause burning sensations in the eyes. In some diseases the patient may experience colored vision, in which the world may appear weakly or strongly tinted. Red vision may follow retinal hemorrhage or snow blindness. Yellow vision may follow digitalis or quinine poisoning. Green vision may be caused by wounds of the cornea. Blue vision has been reported in cases of alcoholism. In tobacco scotoma the vision may be reddish or greenish.

Before the universal practice of vaccination, about 35 per cent of blindness was due to smallpox. Today, according to one medical authority, 2 per cent of eye diseases may be traced to syphilis. Mumps, measles, scarlet fever, ulcers, and sinus infections may all attack the eye. Methyl alcohol may cause complete blindness.

Range of Vision

Light sensitivity from the feeble twinkle of a star to full sunlight may be in the order of 1,000,000 to one — a remarkably great range that far exceeds that of any "electric eye" or mechanism. Again, tests of the speed of vision show that mere fractions of a second are enough for the eye — and the brain — to record stimuli and to grasp significance and meaning in fairly complicated fields of view. As to detail, Ralph M. Evans writes, "A telephone wire may be seen at a distance greater than a quarter of a mile." Although an image that small could hardly be recorded by a glass lens and a photographic plate measuring less than 1/16 inch in diameter (the area covered by the fovea, see below), the eye is able to perform the feat.

Anomalies of Seeing

Near the fovea of the retina is a "blind spot," where the optic nerve of the eye connects. Located slightly inward toward the nose near the center of the retina, it points out obliquely toward the world. At a close distance the blind spot covers a relatively small area in the field of view. At seven feet, this area measures eight inches across and increases its spread into distance. Looking into the sky it covers a region about eleven times the size of the moon. Although the eye sees nothing at this point, a person is seldom

+

With the left eye closed, stare with the right eye at the cross to the left. Move the page slowly toward the eye; at one point the imp will disappear. Where the retinal nerves connect to form the main optic nerve, there is a blind spot.

conscious of emptiness or blackness. The brain, in fact, "fills in" with whatever happens to be in the environment. While you are reading this book, the blind spot will presumably "see" type matter.

Many industrial injuries and road accidents while driving at night may be traced to the blind spot, for if objects are in direct line with it, a person may not be aware of them.

In viewing objects and colors there is a certain amount of retinal lag. Motion pictures are thus made possible, for the picture of each frame lags and carries over into the next as if continuous. Incidentally, off-focus movies are tiring to the eye because its mechanism of vision may struggle to clarify the image without success, straining the muscles of accommodation and causing distress.

When the eye scans space, it does so in skips and hops. Otherwise vision would be blurred. More than this, in viewing a color, there is a tendency on the part of the eye to bring up an afterimage of the complement. Upon

The afterimage. Stare at the center of the black disk for about 30 seconds. Then transfer attention to the black dot at the right. A bright afterimage will be seen. With colors, the afterimage will be complementary in hue.

staring at an area of red for about thirty seconds, blue-green will be seen. Yellow and ultramarine blue are thus complementary, as are purple and yellow-green, orange and turquoise blue.

Recent scientific experiments indicate that afterimage effects take place in the brain rather than in the eye itself. Hypnotized subjects have been able to "see" afterimages despite the fact that the retinas of their eyes have been stimulated by suggestion only.

Foveal Vision

Most of the action of seeing takes place in a relatively small area called the fovea. Here is where the eye has a good sense of detail, color, and form. As an experiment, look into a mirror at the tip of your nose and observe that, with the attention so fixed, it becomes next to impossible to count your own teeth. In perimetry the areas of sensitivity to detail and color may be charted. Indeed, the outer boundary of vision — sensitive chiefly to brightness and motion — may have its sensitivity lessened by fatigue and disease. Here again occupational hazard may be encountered.

Ordinarily, the smallest area of sensitivity to color is for green, then red, then yellow and blue. Where such fields may be oddly distributed, disease and even mental disturbance may be diagnosed. Persons with neurotic tendencies, for example, may have abnormally arranged color fields.

Foveal and peripheral vision differ. There is indeed a sort of double process of seeing. A golfer with the foveal area of his eye on the ball will

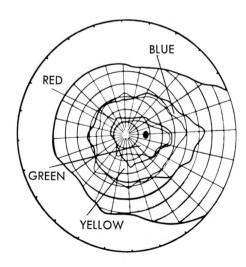

The color fields of the retina. Only the center of the eye is sensitive to color. The smallest area of response is for green, the largest for blue.

use the peripheral field to guide the arc of his club. The ball player will do likewise. The prizefighter may concentrate on the chin of his adversary and yet be alert to "haymakers" swinging in from the side.

Vision and the Other Senses

It has long been known that the stimulation of color will produce reactions throughout the human organism and that the activity of one sense organ will influence another. Sherrington has written, "All parts of the nervous system are connected together and no part of it is probably ever capable of reaction without affecting and being affected by various other parts, and it is a system certainly never absolutely at rest." There may be suppression of sensation or activation of it. Popcorn may not have much taste if eaten while riding on a roller coaster. An effort to hear at night in the woods will seem to sharpen the sense of sight as well as the sense of hearing.

In 1931 Karl Zietz reported an unusual phenomenon relating to color and sound. While tones of high pitch or low pitch were sounded small areas of color were exposed to the eye for a fraction of a second. Sounds of low pitch tended to shift the appearance of colors toward an adjacent deeper hue. Sounds of high pitch tended to shift them toward adjacent lighter hues. Thus low pitch tones had the effect of making red appear deeper or more bluish; orange became reddish; yellow became brownish and sometimes reddish; green became bluer; blue became more like violet. High pitch tones gave red an apparent yellowish or orange cast; orange shifted toward yellow; yellow became paler; green became yellowish; blue seemed lighter and greener.

In 1935 a Russian scientist, S. V. Kravkov, published a further series of intriguing data and conclusions on the effect of sound upon the color sensibility of the eye. Kravkov's observers were seated in a dark room before a spectroscope. Sounds were transmitted to their ears by means of telephone receivers. After the eye of an observer had been adapted to the light and after a check had been made on his particular sensibility to the hues of the spectrum, sounds were poured into his ears. Another check was then made. Kravkov reports, " The cone sensibility to the rays of the green-blue parts of the spectrum *rises* under the action of a simultaneous sound, whereas the sensibility to the yellow-orange-red parts of the spectrum *decreases*."

The work of Kravkov has been repeated and extended by Frank Allen and Manuel Schwartz of Canada. These two men have confirmed the same findings and have also studied the effect of the stimulation of taste and smell upon color perception. Using an aqueous solution of sulfate of quinine, which has a bitter taste, red sensation was depressed and green sensation was increased. Sugar had no apparent visual effect.

As to the sense of smell, "With the odor of oil of geranium as the stimulating substance, the red and violet sensations . . . were depressed in sensitivity and the green enhanced."

Estimates of Time, Length, Weight

Mental judgments of common tasks may also be influenced by color. According to Kurt Goldstein, under the influence of red light, time is likely to be overestimated. Conversely, under the influence of green or blue light, time is likely to be underestimated. In the functional application of color, cool hues would thus seem best where routine and monotonous tasks are performed, such as in offices and factories. Warm hues would be suitable for living rooms, restaurants, and cocktail lounges — where time in apparent "slow motion" might be more pleasurable.

Similarly, "Estimation of the length of sticks based on visual touch stimulation is much less correct in red light. The threshold is lower in green and enlarged in red stimulation." In other words, things are likely to seem longer and bigger under warm light, and shorter and smaller under cool light.

Results of the same nature are encountered in estimations of weights. Under red light, weights will be judged as heavier; under green light they will be judged as lighter. Again, functional applications for color would suggest the use of light, cool colors on boxes and containers which must be carried about in workaday activities.

Eyestrain

Without going into elaborate detail, the causes of eyestrain may be listed as follows:

Glare.
Excessive contrasts within the field of view.
Distressing brightness and motion on the outer boundaries of vision.
Prolonged convergence of the eyes on near objects.
Constant pupillary adjustments from light to dark.
Continual shifts in accommodation from near to far.
Lack of convenient and pleasing areas for visual relaxation.

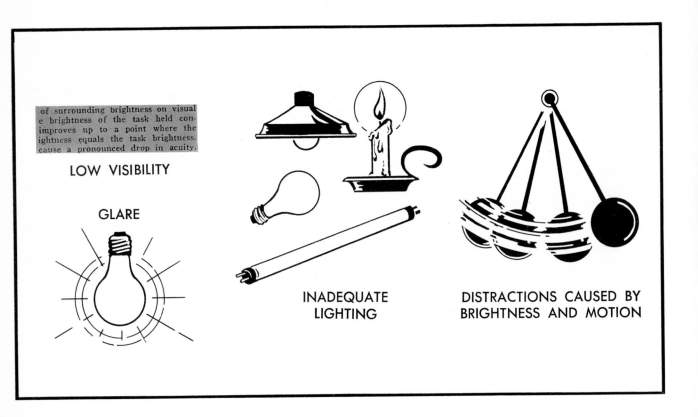

LOW VISIBILITY

GLARE

INADEQUATE
LIGHTING

DISTRACTIONS CAUSED BY
BRIGHTNESS AND MOTION

The causes of eyestrain.

Eyestrain — or what the doctor frequently prefers to call ocular fatigue — is muscular. The retina itself unless exposed to extremely high intensities is not easily tired. Trouble is related more to efforts at accommodation, muscular imbalance, and the like. Where the eye may be abused, the following adverse reactions are to be noted, all of which are measurable with instruments:

Severe dilation of the pupil during course of work.
Higher rate of blinking.
Collapse of the nerves on the outer boundaries of the retina.
Increased muscular tension.
Increased nervousness and fatigue.
Nausea and psychological irritability.

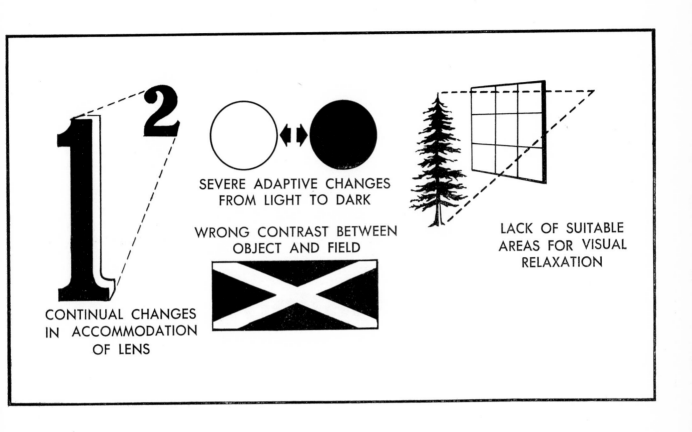

SEVERE ADAPTIVE CHANGES
FROM LIGHT TO DARK

WRONG CONTRAST BETWEEN
OBJECT AND FIELD

LACK OF SUITABLE
AREAS FOR VISUAL
RELAXATION

CONTINUAL CHANGES
IN ACCOMMODATION
OF LENS

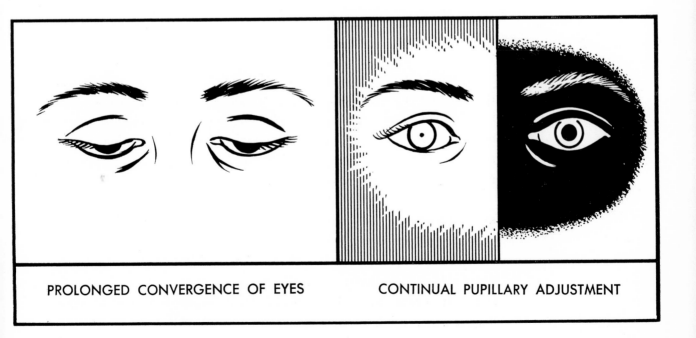

PROLONGED CONVERGENCE OF EYES   CONTINUAL PUPILLARY ADJUSTMENT

3

Problems of

Illumination

Seeing is very much a dynamic process. Prominent psychologists have noted that the sensory system and the motor system of the human body are not separate and distinct. On the contrary, they seem to be parts of a major, comprehensive system, and their pathways connect. A person does not see only with his eye and brain; the reactions of vision involve the body as a whole.

In lighting and color research, two divergent views are held by certain illuminating engineers and medical authorities. One argument insists that high levels of light are the need and the answer to good vision (which they no doubt are), while many opthalmologists plead for caution and warn, through clinical experience, that light can be a damaging thing where it is not properly utilized and controlled.

The author is frank to state that his prejudice, if any, is in favor of the more conservative viewpoint. During his years of experience he has encountered numerous examples of too much light and too much glare. Furthermore, he is convinced that the whole science of illumination stands on the threshold of a new order. Vision is not a simple, optical reaction to light; it involves complex physiological and psychological factors which men are only now beginning to appreciate.

Decorative and functional lighting in one dramatic installation. General Assembly at United Nations, New York. (Ezra Stoller photograph.)

A good example of an "egg-crate" ceiling which creates a bright, even illumination, with glare cut off by the ceiling baffles.

The German Weight Lifters!

Werner has called attention to an unusual experiment in which a dog, forced to lie at rest, was unable to learn the difference between a circle and a triangle. When the animal was permitted to move about, however, the problem was quickly solved. All too clearly, vision may be influenced by mind, mental effort, body function, and reaction. To say that man needs a certain measure of light, that ratios of brightness should lie within fixed limits, is merely a small part of the truth.

If light can aid seeing, it also at times may actually impair human performance. Consider a rather curious tale told by a psychologist. In a competition among German weight lifters, existing records were not equalled in a certain auditorium. As reported by C. H. G. Hartgenbusch, the hall in which the competition took place was brilliantly illuminated, presumably with rows of lighting fixtures and exposed electric lamp bulbs. To all indications, this distraction made it difficult for the weight lifters to concentrate on their task and to find a point in view on which they might fix their eyes. Weight lifting, like so many jobs, requires a certain bodily stability. When good orientation and coordination are upset — as by blinding light — the body finds difficulty in functioning at its best. The reader may recall that he, too, has at times closed his eyes (to eliminate sight of his environment) when attempting some tough mental or muscular exertion. Like the German weight lifters, he also has wanted to rid himself of distractions that might take his mind off his effort.

Light Levels

Not so many years ago a sizable portion of the lighting profession held to the questionable belief that the answer to good visibility was directly related to light intensity in terms of footcandles. Casual seeing required few footcandles; critical seeing demanded many.

However, light levels themselves do not have the importance which many investigators attach to them. Simonson and Brozek in a series of tests concluded that many lighting engineers tended to exaggerate the importance of illumination level. They failed to note much difference in visual fatigue under light levels ranging from 5 to 300 footcandles. After a very thorough investigation involving acuity, threshold size, accommodation, convergence, brightness discrimination, and nine instrumental measurements, they concluded that fatigue seemed more related to the difficulty of the task than to light level. In other words, the eyes tired chiefly when they had something difficult to do. Illumination was by no means the all-important factor. Given what might be termed adequate light (around 50 footcandles), illumination levels beyond this did not lessen fatigue to any appreciable degree.

In support of the above, the following statement by Ferree and Rand will probably meet with the approval of anyone who has made a devout study of illumination. It involves a point too often overlooked by many proponents of high light levels. "If, for example, the light is well distributed in the field of vision and there are no extremes of surface brightness, our tests seem to indicate that the eye, so far as the problem of lighting is concerned, is practically independent of intensity. That is, when the proper distribution effects are obtained, intensities high enough to give maximum discrimination of detail may be employed without causing appreciable damage or discomfort to the eye."

Unless there is proper control of light through control of brightness and color in the environment, light level alone is an insufficient criterion.

How Much Light?

Ophthalmologists know that most visual tasks may be performed with good skill under widely different light intensities. Starting with total darkness there is a sharp rise in seeing ability when two or three footcandles are reached. Efficiency will continue to rise *until a level of about 30 footcandles is attained*. This becomes more or less of an optimum level, for beyond 30 footcandles the curve of visual efficiency levels off sharply. For still higher efficiency, light levels must be tripled or quadrupled.

The English speak of high efficiency (about 90 per cent) with relatively low light levels of 30 footcandles or less. Where 95 per cent or more efficiency may be necessary, levels up to 1500 footcandles may be required.

Here, however, medical authorities differ with many lighting engineers. There is a tendency in this country to claim the need for brilliant *general* illumination and to imply (speciously) that a good job of illumination is not achieved until the *entire room* is a blaze of light. This viewpoint is both hazardous and erroneous. To draw a comparison, one may equally contend that a heating system should be designed to assure a 72 degree temperature at twenty below zero and that this heating system should be operated at full blast regardless of weather conditions. A far more sensible and economical view has been set forth by H. C. Weston. He speaks of efficiency in relation to light level. If an accuracy of 90 per cent in some complex task may require over 1,000 footcandles, Weston remarks that this light may well be

With increase in illumination, seeing improves sharply up to a level of about 30 or 35 footcandles. This level is optimum for average tasks. For added visual efficiency, light levels may have to be increased many times.

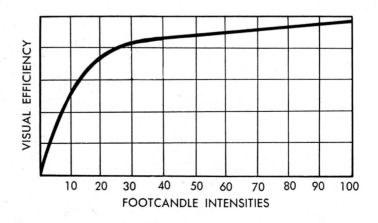

VISUAL EFFICIENCY

10 20 30 40 50 60 70 80 90 100

FOOTCANDLE INTENSITIES

concentrated over the task and not spread throughout the room. This would mean economy in fixture use and power consumption; also, a blaze of light around and away from the task may actually create unnecessary glare and visual distraction.

In simple words, 30 to 35 footcandles constitute an ideal level for countless seeing tasks in offices, factories and schools. Intensities above this up to 50 or 75 footcandles or so may be tolerated if the cost of installation and maintenance is not excessive. Yet if particularly critical tasks are undertaken, concentrated *local light sources* should be added rather than the entire area illuminated. Although such practice may raise the eyebrows of some lighting engineers, let the reader be assured that the medical profession by and large will be in accord.

Soft lighting in an auditorium of the Upjohn Company, with walls in an interesting three-tone effect to assure a soft field of view. Courtesy of The Austin Company. (Hedrich-Blessing photograph.)

The solarium in the Ochsner Foundation Hospital, New Orleans, Louisiana, shows the use of vertical slats to diffuse natural light. Ellerbe & Co., architects. Courtesy of Thru-Vu Vertical Blind Corp. (Miller-Callaway photograph.)

High Brightness

What are the dangers of glare and high brightness? LeGrand H. Hardy and Gertrude Rand have written: "The effect of changes of illumination on ocular fatigue in the zones ordinarily encountered, that is, between 10 and 30 footcandles, is relatively unimportant. It is certain that continued use of the eyes, especially for fine work, under values of an order of 1 per cent of these intensities will result in eyestrain and functional inefficiency, with possible organic damage. A corresponding increase in these intensities to hundredfold values of artificial illumination will probably also result in eyestrain and ocular fatigue unless adjustment is made in the quality and distribution of the light."

The author has encountered far more complaints about "strong" light than about "weak" light. This is particularly true these days when high levels may be readily achieved with fluorescent sources. Lighting engineers are well aware of this. L. D. Morgan has pointed out that lighting engineers cannot shrug off complaints of bad lighting by insisting that the critics are being emotional rather than rational. Imagined or not, people who suffer for their feelings may experience just as much pain as those who have a bodily injury. Illumination must be psychologically as well as visually acceptable.

High brightness (produced either by lighting fixtures or by brightly illuminated colors of high reflectance) has been the subject of many patent conclusions and tends to verify the statement that 60 per cent reflectance for wall areas is a good upper limit. Luckiesh, one of America's leading authorities on illumination, reached the conclusion that brightness around a task ought to be lower than that of the central field. Many of his experiments showed high surrounding brightness to be definitely objectionable. The same

Birren's Principle. High levels of illumination seem tolerable only where there are small brightness differences in the field of view. Where reflectances (walls, floors, equipment) have excessive differences in light and dark, moderate light seems necessary for comfort. The chart expresses this in a general way.

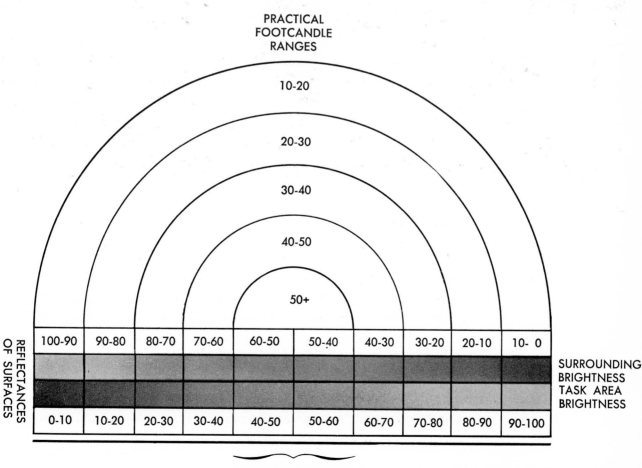

view has been upheld by Ferree and Rand. The presence of high brightness around the task tends to cause the eyes not only to look up and away, but to adjust and accommodate to the brightness. As a result, if deliberate effort is required to reject the environment and concentrate on the task, fatigue may be rapid and the eyes may lose much of their power to see clearly.

Again, there are definite psychologic factors to be noted. D. B. Harmon has observed that the human organism tends to orient itself to the brightest area in its environment. High brightness may condition the body for muscular activity and so make mental and more sedentary activity difficult if not impossible. Physical tasks may well be performed in a brilliant environment, but tasks requiring severe mental and visual concentration are best performed against softer and less aggressive backgrounds.

In a generously lighted interior where walls and furnishings are all on the brilliant side, the psychologic make-up of an individual may unconsciously rebel at confining and sedentary tasks. In the emotional sense, extreme room brightness tends to draw attention to the room at large, to invite a wandering interest. More suppressed colors draw attention to details within the room and set up effective aids to concentration on them.

To quote once again from Ferree and Rand, "The eye has grown up under daylight. Under this condition only three adjustments have developed, and indeed only three are needed: the reaction of the pupil to regulate the amount of light entering the eye and to aid the lens in focusing the light from objects at different distances, and accommodation and convergence to bring the object on the principal axis of the lens and the image on the fovea. . . . . " These adjustments tend to be co-ordinated. When they are separated, trouble is encountered. High brightness in the field of view, if isolated from the task, may cause disruption. The eye will thereupon struggle to set things right. *"This striving to clear up its vision by ineffectual maladjustments is the cause of what is commonly called eyestrain."*

There is good reason for architects and designers to be wary of extremely high light levels and of an overabundance of white and off-white colors. Seeing may be handicapped, the eye may be damaged, and psychological distraction may cause serious emotional disturbances.

Colored Light

There have been many recent objections to fluorescent light. Empirically it seems to have an "unreal" quality which may seem unpleasant. Fluorescent light has what is called a "band" rather than a "continuous" spectrum. It

Illumination may be vastly improved through the simple application of a coat of paint, as indicated in the before and after photographs shown here.

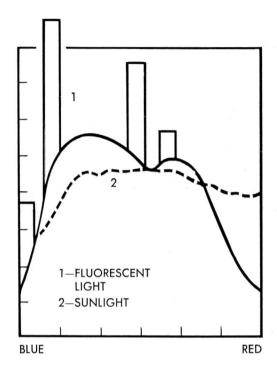

1—FLUORESCENT
LIGHT
2—SUNLIGHT

BLUE   RED

Natural light (2) has what is known as a "continuous spectrum" and contains some amounts of all colors. Fluorescent light (1) emits a "band" spectrum and has sharp peaks and pits.

transmits light only in certain regions of the spectrum, not in all of them as do sunlight, daylight, and incandescent light. With the introduction of red phosphors, however, the quality of fluorescent light has been vastly improved and more red radiation — so flattering to human appearance — now makes fluorescent light more "agreeable."

The eye has different sensitivity under different conditions of illumination. In the light-adapted eye, the spectrum is brightest at yellow and yellow-green. In the dark-adapted eye, the spectrum is brightest at blue-green, and red may fade out into blackness. In comparable fashion, the eye will have a different acuity when its field of view is illuminated by lights of different hue.

Generally speaking, the eye sees well in natural light equivalent to daylight. Acuity is reduced as the spectral quality approaches blue. It is substantially high (perhaps even increased) as the spectral quality approaches yellow and orange — but not so far as red.

Some claims have been presented for artificial "daylight" sources (decidedly greenish and bluish). It is said to increase the apparent distinctness of certain objects, an observation that perhaps has some merit. However, a yellowish quality in a light source is far easier to explain and defend from the standpoint of acuity. Luckiesh points out that yellow is the region of maximum selectivity, the brightest portion of the spectrum. It is without aberration (that is, the eye normally focuses it perfectly), and it is psychologically pleasing. By experiment, Luckiesh also demonstrated that by filtering out blue and violet radiation in a mercury light or in a tungsten lamp, visual acuity remained practically constant, despite the reduced amount of light absorbed by the filter. This would mean that, as far as visual acuity is concerned, yellow has definite advantages. Sodium light, for example, is highly efficient, although its distortion of colors makes it impossible for use under many circumstances.

Ferree and Rand placed yellow illumination at the top of the list, orange-yellow second, followed by yellow-green and green. Deep red, blue, and violet were least desirable. Blue, in fact, is very difficult for the eye to focus and will cause objects to appear blurred and surrounded by halos.

Under extreme dark adaptation, however, the eye seems to have best acuity under red light. Red illumination has been widely used for instrument panels in airplanes, for control rooms on ships and submarines. It has little influence on the dark-adapted eye and is not, in fact, easily seen on the outer boundaries of the retina, where the cones are lacking. It is therefore suitable as a blackout illuminant and will fail to stimulate the eye except when its rays strike near the fovea.

Conclusions

Footcandle levels from 25 to 50 are satisfactory for most tasks (about 30 or 35 footcandles are optimum). Where higher levels are employed, color and brightness must be "smoothed out" to avoid excessive contrasts. Proofreading areas, for example, may have general illumination up to 100 or more footcandles if walls, floors, and equipment, tables, and the like are relatively pale in tone.

If a lighting system is such that it exposes the eye to great extremes in light and dark (possibly bright overhead fixtures and dark floors and equipment), constant pupillary adjustments will necessitate a lot of light on the task itself for the eye to "fight" its way through the extremes. However, if uniformity of brightness is apparent — and eye adjustments unnecessary — the eye can actually see better and more clearly under relatively dim light (footcandles to the contrary).

The indirect lighting system (also the so-called luminous ceiling) is desirable and appropriate in offices, for example, and is usually psychologically appealing. The best type of fixture is one with an opalescent bowl or reflector which will transmit an intensity of light that approximately matches the brightness reflected by the ceiling, thus blending fixture and ceiling into one relatively uniform area. Such fixtures are made for both incandescent and fluorescent sources. Indirect light (semi-indirect in the above instance) seems to be "easy" on the eyes. It effectively reduces shadows and specular reflections. The room appears "cheerful," lacking in harshness, and vision may operate efficiently under reasonable footcandle levels.

However, when floors or equipment are unusually dark, the ceiling overhead in the indirect lighting system may become a glare source. This is no fault of the system. By using lighter colors on floors, desks, and furnishings, more uniformity will be realized (and more footcandles because of multiple reflections). The system will be at its best.

Indirect lighting systems (at least in the author's experience) are the safest of all to assure visual comfort. They are not efficient from the lighting standpoint because the bulbs or tubes are concealed and light distribution must depend chiefly upon reflectance. Turn the reflectors around, expose the bulbs or tubes, and footcandle readings will jump — but visual efficiency may simultaneously collapse.

The direct lighting system requires expert care and engineering. In industrial plants having monitors, high bays, or exceedingly high ceilings, this method of illumination is generally the only practical one. In certain machine operations it holds the added advantage of giving form and shape to materials or products (indirect light tends to "wash out" highlights and shadows).

The fault with many direct lighting systems is that the eye is too frequently exposed to "naked" bulbs or tubes. They may stand out in marked contrast

with a dark ceiling or overhead, thus raising havoc with the principle of uniformity. The conventional type of RLM reflector is often inadequate. With deeper shields or reflectors, baffles, diffusing lenses, and the like, glare may be reduced and the eye less bothered. When the reflectors are near the ceiling, they should be painted white on top to blend with the overhead. Obviously, machines and floors should be as light as possible, both to reflect more light and to reduce brightness differences.

Further, when the task demands critical use of the eyes to distinguish fine details, supplementary light sources (over and above the direct or indirect lighting system) may be necessary. Some tasks require a lot of light. Yet, as ever, the surroundings should be kept as uniform as possible in brightness.

4

Academic

Harmony

The author is frank to state that in his experience academic systems of color harmony hold little appeal. Carefully schooled in the Brewsterian theory, in the conclusions of Chevreul, Munsell, and Ostwald, he has found that the arbitrary and orthodox method of color arrangement lacks an all-important verification in actual human experience.

Where the concords follow carefully plotted mathematical order, the eye may see neatness and regularity, but beauty itself in the emotional sense may be less evident. It has been proposed, for example, that color schemes are harmonious if their hues and areas will (through color-wheel measurement) cancel each other and form neutral gray. Yet a combination of mustard yellow and lavender will also cancel into neutral gray! In other theories, complex and elaborate graduations, contrasts, balances are sought on a mathematical basis through laborious effort. Yet the result may have the precise tidiness of an arithmetic table and be equally vapid.

When the public is to be enthralled, no formal system of color arrangement can safely disregard psychological factors and innate preferences! Beauty is a subjective experience and not an objective fact. As a case in point, all academic color systems state without exception that complimentary colors are harmonious. Are they? The top favorites of most persons are red and blue. Yet red finds its true complement in blue-green, while blue finds its opposite in a yellowish orange. He who would argue that color schemes composed of red and blue-green or blue and yellowish orange are superior to a simple arrangement of red and blue will reach a false conclusion.

Generalities are what are needed, coupled with a good knowledge of principles which have actually stood the test of public approval. Yet even here many architects, designers, and decorators are sadly lacking in enlightenment.

Simple Color Form

There are a few simple principles of color and color harmony which might be termed "scientific" for the reason that they involve an almost universal appeal. Study the Color Triangle in the chapter "Color Organization." In human sensation the three primary forms are pure color, white, and black. The secondary forms are gray, tint, shade, tone. Tints are whitish colors, shades are blackish, and tones are grayish. If it is part of the psychological make-up of people to see the world of color in this way, to sort out all visual experiences into seven compact "boxes," then a plausible deduction is to be reached. One principle to be noted is that individual colors should always be lucid; they should have clarity and be examples of perfection in their particular classifications.

Pure colors, if chosen, should be truly pure, brilliant, and as saturated as possible.

Whites should be unquestionably white and blacks unquestionably black. (A color such as white used for building exteriors, however, may require some shading to avoid glare. Yet in interiors and in architectural decoration the above point is applicable.)

Grays, tints, shades, and tones, when chosen, should all be unmistakable as such and should not be confused with other forms.

Many practical examples of the above principle may be quoted. With white, for example, dingy tones are likely to appear dirty and unattractive. (Tints of blue are often added to white pigments to emphasize whiteness.)

Similarly, any color should ordinarily shun the in-between stigma. A red slightly modified with white may appear faded and weak. Yet a red modified with enough white to lift its classification out of purity and into the crisp charm of pink may find its beauty restored.

In the case of orange, a slightly blackish cast may make it seem dirty and soiled. Enough black would shift it to brown, and here, as another form, it may again delight the eye.

Orderly Arrangements

The pure colors of the spectrum divide themselves into warmth (red, orange, yellow), and coolness (green, blue, violet). Two colors seem to have neutral "temperature" (yellow-green and red-violet). While color circles exist by the score, not all agree with each other. Some complement red with green, others red with blue-green. Some are planned with three primaries, red-yellow-blue; Ostwald uses red-yellow-green-blue at equidistant points; Munsell uses red-yellow-green-blue-purple.

Color systems too frequently feature rules that are unhappily academic. In the early part of the nineteenth century M. Chevreul of France devised a series of "propositions" which have become somewhat classical in discussions of color harmony.

Complementary assortments are superior to all others.

Primary colors assort better than secondaries.

Colors which appear none too harmonious side by side may be improved by a white or black outline or separation.

A primary color (red, yellow, blue) combines better with two secondaries (orange, green, violet) than a secondary combines with two primaries.

Black harmonizes effectively with deep colors such as blue and violet, while white looks best with light colors such as yellow, orange and green.

Where light and dark colors may be used together, gray may be an ideal ground.

It was Chevreul who devised the system of working in terms of complements, split-complements, adjacents, and triads, still currently taught in art education.

However, psychological inquiry would speak in even simpler terms. J. P. Guilford writes, "There is some evidence that either very small or very large differences in hue give more pleasing results than do medium differences." Parry Moon and D. E. Spencer have reached a similar conclusion. In orderly arrangements of color, pleasing combinations are found when the intervals between any two colors are "unambiguous." Refer to the chart included herewith. If the chosen color is yellow, for example, all other colors occupying the shaded area would be ambiguous (and unpleasant), while all other colors occupying the clear areas would be unambiguous or pleasant. Thus the two shaded sections immediately next to the chosen yellow — orange-yellow and greenish-yellow — would be unpleasant. In the next two sections, orange and yellow-green would be found and here harmony would be restored. In the two next large shaded sections — red and green — am-

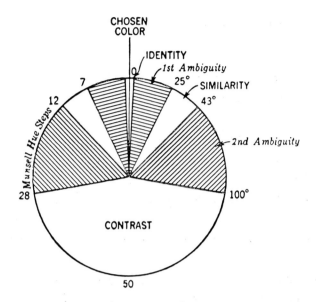

CHOSEN
COLOR

IDENTITY
1st Ambiguity
25°
SIMILARITY
43°

2nd Ambiguity

CONTRAST

7
12
28
100°
50

Munsell Hue Steps

Most persons seem to prefer color arrangements based either on analogy or on contrast — the white areas, left. Less appeal is found in other relationships — the shaded areas, left. After Moon and Spencer.

biguity would once more be encountered. The complementary region of the chart would offer unambiguous and therefore free harmony.

The same general reactions — and the same general arrangement of the chart — would hold true for other key colors chosen from the color circle. "Pleasing intervals and ambiguous intervals exist between colors, and an orderly geometric arrangement of color points leads to harmony."

Further Observations

A person is likely to see harmony either in colors that are closely related or in those that are antithetical or opposite — and not in other relationships. This conclusion suggests two big guiding principles, *analogy* and *contrast*. To these the author takes the liberty of adding a third principle, *balance*.

Analogy is of an emotional nature, bringing together colors which bear close resemblance to each other and which give preference to one section of the color circle. For this reason, analogous schemes are either warm or cool in feeling. They are desirable in architectural decoration because they tend to hold together as a unit.

Contrast is more visual. It is particularly useful where large areas are to be complemented — furnishings contrasted against walls, architectural elements spaced well apart.

Balance means a fuller diet of the spectrum. Combinations of red, yellow, green, blue include both analogy and contrast and are traditional and appropriate to decorative treatments and large scale color plans.

Another seemingly natural law of color harmony has been noted by I. H. Godlove. He writes, "If we note the lightnesses which are exhibited by mixtures of common pigments of 20 successive hues at their levels of greatest vividness, beginning with yellow and proceeding through green, blue, purple, red and back to yellow, we find the following well-marked sequence. The lightness goes down toward the greens, is lowest at purple-blue, and comes up again through red to yellow."

As far as average reaction is concerned, combinations of color usually seem to be concordant and pleasing when the above sequence is respected — that is, when light tones of colors which in normal purity are light are combined with deep tones of colors which in normal purity are dark.

To make Godlove's observation clear, in combining tints, shades, and tones, the hue normally high in value should have the lighter tint, and the hue normally low in value should have the deeper tint or shade. Here are a few examples.

Deep blue looks better with pale green than deep green looks with pale blue.

Orange buff (peach) looks better with deep violet than lavender looks with brown (which is a deep shade of orange).

Pink looks better with dark blue or purple than lavender or pale blue look with maroon.

Pale yellow looks better with brown or blue or violet, than any pale greens, blues or lavenders would look with olive drab (which is a deep shade of yellow).

Modified Colors

There is excellent order in the organization of the Color Triangle previously described. In the sequence of modified colors (tints, shades, tones), any straight path on the Triangle leads to a concordant beauty. The reader will probably agree with the following points.

First of all, as already mentioned, pure colors look well with white and black. Primary hues (red, yellow, blue, green) seem to have architectural stability and to be direct, frank, and obvious in their impression. Intermediate hues (yellow-green, blue-green, purples) have more subtlety and hence tend to be more exclusive and refined.

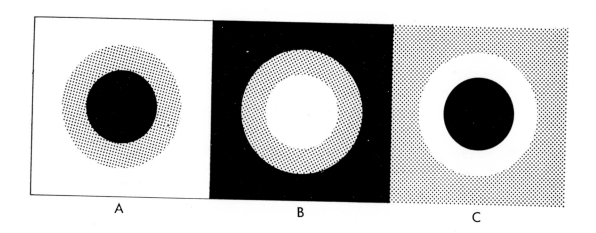

A   B   C

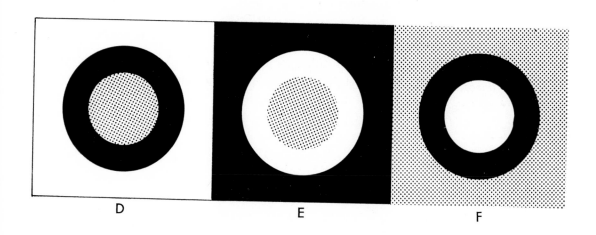

D   E   F

Orderly sequence in color values seems to be most pleasing. Arrangements A and B above appear more coherent than the others.

The secondary forms (tints, shades, tones, gray) also tend to look well together.

White, gray, and black are likewise harmonious.

Pure color, tint, and white combine well together.

Pure color, shade, and black are harmonious.

Harmony is also found in diagonal paths. Tints harmonize with tones and black. Shades harmonize with tones and white. Pure colors harmonize with tones and gray.

Any remarks about the Color Triangle, however, are general and theoretical. Yet there is good reason for harmony, the Triangle expressing a natural order of color sequence.

The Balance of Values

The quality of value in color has very much of an architectural quality. Colors are of different weight and appear light or heavy in direct relation to their apparent brightness or reflectance.

To make a simple point, study the illustrations on value. The eye is quick to see neatness and order in equally stepped intervals. Where values are close, they tend to blend together as one visual unit. Architectural form and decoration frequently tend to "fall apart" when such balance is not properly achieved.

5

Color and

Form

A rchitecture and decoration constantly deal with form. The two should be integral wherever possible. "Architecture is a plastic thing," says Le Corbusier. Color can make it even more so. However, form has frequently been approached with too little regard for color and color itself has been looked upon as something superficial and applied.

The history of modern architecture has been greatly dominated by form. Even the classicists have stripped hue from Greek and Roman styles. Among modernists, color has been handled in a primitive and almost childish way. Pretensions may have been disdained, but where on occasion color has been used, the viewpoint has usually been obvious, audacious but seldom original or creative. Frank Lloyd Wright has used naturalism with the sentimentality of a Thoreau, presumably distrusting color as an expression of unwarranted egocentricity. World's fairs have been unimaginatively adorned with the most elementary of colors. Reactions from marble and limestone have been impulsive more than inventive.

Gestalt Psychology

The fact that clarity of color is most appealing seems to apply also to three-dimensional form. A square or cube may appear to be ungainly and awkward when slightly elongated in shape. Yet in the rectangle and ovoid shape beauty is again evident. Elaborate principles have been deducted from classical architecture by Jay Hambidge in his dynamic symmetry, while Rutherford Boyd has applied mathematical formulas to parabolic curves. If these studies are academic they are also scholarly and hold considerable interest.

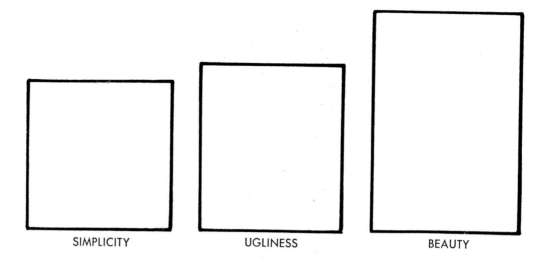

SIMPLICITY UGLINESS BEAUTY

Good order in form seems to require simplicity and clarity of shape or mass. Slight distortions of familiar areas seem to be visually disturbing.

Gestalt psychology is not an easy science to define. It deals with perception as a coordinated unity of impressions and not as a group of separated or isolated parts. A square, for example, is more than four equal straight lines; it is a unity, complete in itself. As David Katz writes, "The whole is more than the sum of its separate parts." This *more* lies in the interpretation of the human mind. Because this branch of psychology is very much concerned with human conceptions of form, the whole visual process has come under its careful surveillance.

According to Katz, "As a general principle it may be stated that the more primitive a form is, the more closely it will be tied up with emotion." That simplicity and clarity are unconsciously sought by the eye is evident in the fact that slightly irregular or distorted forms will appear quite regular in their afterimages. Further, an irregular form seen for a short fraction of time will not appear as such, for the eye will simplify its shape and contour.

Broken forms and broken lines tend to appear unbroken. The more obvious the form, the more it resists alteration by the observer. A straight line is a more stable structure than a broken one. The delineation of a circle will be more easily seen as a line than will the delineation of a triangle. Arcs demand their continuation more strongly than do straight lines.

Experience is also vital. Such modern forms of painting as non-objectivism and surrealism may confuse the naive observer. If familiarity produces any change of attitude, one must recognize that study and training are important factors in the shaping of human taste. Yet there is no doubt but that some forms have more universal qualities than others. Probably Le Corbusier had this in mind when he stated, "Primary forms are beautiful forms because they can be clearly appreciated."

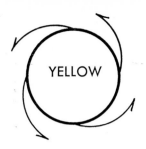

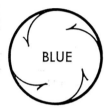

Kandinsky's conception of color and motion. Yellow expands; blue contracts; red is stable.

Hard and Soft Colors

To the Gestalt psychologist red and orange colors are "hard," while green and blue colors are "soft." Colors of short wave length mix better with a gray of similar value and tend to "melt" with it. Colors of long wave length, however, segregate more clearly. This phenomenon involves optics as well as mental interpretation, as will be described.

The abstract painter Kandinsky held similar views. He gave the spectrum major dimensions of warmth and coolness, lightness and darkness. Blue and yellow were dominant: "Generally speaking, warmth or cold in color means an approach respectively to yellow or to blue."

Kandinsky saw movement. Yellow had a maximum spreading action, it tended to approach the observer. Blue moved in upon itself and retreated. Red "rings inwardly with a determined and powerful intensity. It glows in itself, maturely, and does not distribute its rigor aimlessly." "Orange is red brought nearer to humanity by yellow." "Violet is red withdrawn from humanity by blue."

It was this painter's belief that "keen" colors (yellow) were best suited to sharp forms, and soft, deep colors (blue) to round forms.

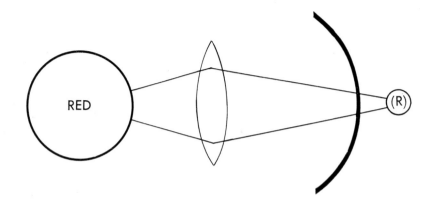

Red colors focus at a point behind the retina. Because the lens of the eye grows convex to pull the image forward, such colors seem nearer and larger. Blue colors focus at a point in front of the retina. Here the lens flattens, pushes the colors back, and makes them appear farther away and smaller.

The Shapes of Colors

Edwin Babbit, a mystic, gave blue the form of the circle, yellow the hexagon and red the triangle. To him the circle, having no corners, represented the tranquillity of blue. The triangle, sturdy and with sharp angles, expressed the energy of red. The hexagon, neither round nor angular, partook of both calmness and vitality.

Possibly a more reasonable association between color and form will be found in the following observations. Because the focus of the eye is not the same for all hues, the colors of the spectrum will appear near or far, large or small accordingly. For example, red focuses normally at a point behind the retina. To see it clearly, the lens of the eye grows convex, pulling the color nearer and thus giving it apparently larger size. On the other hand, blue is focused at a point in front of the retina, causing the lens to flatten out and to push the color back.

Red, orange, and yellow usually form a sharp and clear image on the retina — even through distance and haze — while blue and violet tend to appear blurred. According to W. Allen Wallis, yellow is seen as the largest of colors, then white, red, green, blue, with black smallest of all. A bright image tends to "spread out" over the retina like a drop of water on blotting paper. Thus light colors also appear larger than dark colors.

Red suggests the form of the square and cube. It is hot, dry and opaque in quality. It is solid and substantial and holds a strong attraction. Because it is sharply focused by the eye it lends itself to structural planes and sharp angles.

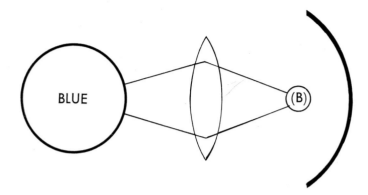

Orange suggests the form of the rectangle. It is less earthly in quality than red, more tinged with a feeling of incandescence. It is warm, dry, compelling. Optically it produces a sharp image and therefore lends itself to angles and to well defined integral ornament.

Yellow suggests the form of the triangle or pyramid with its point or apex down. It is the color of highest visibility in the spectrum and therefore sharp, angular and crisp in quality. Yet is more like light than like substance, more lofty and celestial than mundane.

A simple alliance of color and form.

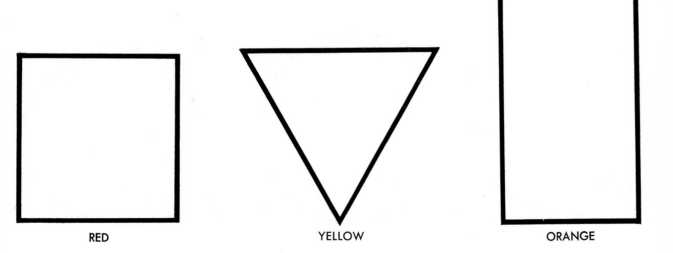

RED   YELLOW   ORANGE

Green suggests the form of the hexagon or icosahedron. It is cool, fresh, soft. It is not sharply focused and therefore does not lend itself to much angularity. Perhaps because of its frequency in nature, green is a big color and can dominate the eye without distressing it.

Blue suggests the form of the circle or sphere. It is cold, wet, transparent, atmospheric. Blue is retiring, dignified, and creates a blurred image in the eye. While it may have bulk, it does not lend itself to sharpness or detail.

Purple suggests the form of the oval. It is somewhat more refined than blue, and the eye also finds difficulty in focusing it. It is soft, filmy, and never angular. Unlike blue, however, it is not so lofty but clings to earth like the distant mountain half hidden in mist.

Physiognomic Perception

In what the Gestalt psychologist terms physiognomic perception, the eye and the brain tend to see more than literally. A mailbox may go unnoticed unless a person is anxious to post a letter. The fact that a mother can identify her child from a long distance is certainly not traceable to her ability to see the youngster's features or even the pattern of his clothing. Architecture and design would reap a rich harvest from a study of physiognomic perception and the magic of it in human experience.

Look over the few simple diagrams presented herewith. In testing the reaction of large groups of individuals, lineal expression seems to have real sense and order. Lines to symbolize such substances as gold, silver, stone are readily interpreted once the material is mentioned. Agreement

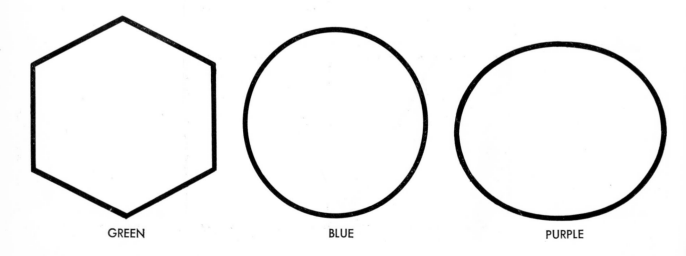

GREEN   BLUE   PURPLE

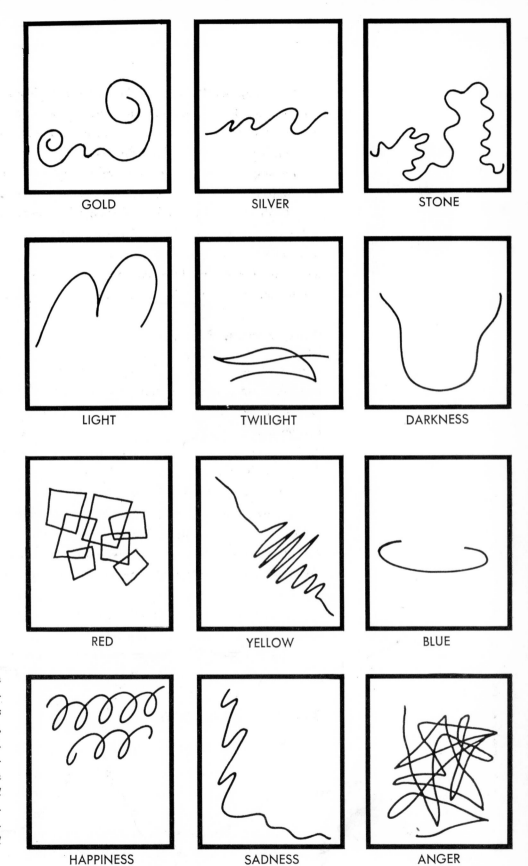

GOLD

SILVER

STONE

LIGHT

TWILIGHT

DARKNESS

RED

YELLOW

BLUE

In the phenomenon known as physiognomic perception, curious relationships are found between words, things, and lineal portrayal. Most persons will see psychological relationships in the above diagrams and legends. Similar associations would exist with architectural forms — a new and fertile field of study.

HAPPINESS

SADNESS

ANGER

Color isolation and diffusion. Equal distribution of black and white in one instance leads to sharp contrast; in the other instance equal distribution leads to grayness.

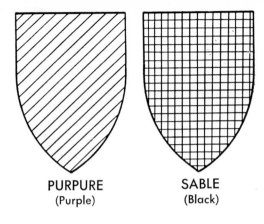

PURPURE
(Purple)

SABLE
(Black)

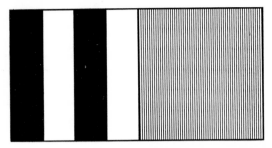

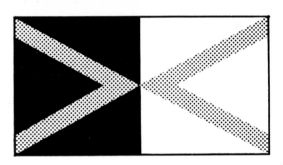

The illusion of brightness contrast. Both gray arrows are the same but look light or dark depending on background contrast.

may run as high as 75 per cent. (The reader may care to test his friends. The substances are to be mentioned by name and the observer asked to identify them with the lineal patterns.)

Forms, designs and patterns may readily be given abstract interpretation, and many modern forms of art seek to exploit them. Illustrated here are simple portrayals of light, twilight, darkness; red, yellow, blue; happiness, sadness, anger. These have been taken from a research study made in Germany by Reinhard Krauss over twenty years ago and partially reported in Heinz Werner's *Comparative Psychology of Mental Development*.

Visibility and Legibility

Brightness is more easily seen than darkness. In light signals, red is the color of highest recognition, followed by green, yellow and white. Blue and purple are difficult to discern. In opaque materials the story is somewhat different. When all colors are seen in the same light, yellow is the most luminous and visible. Orange and red-orange hold maximum attention-value. Blue is likely to be hazy and indistinct. As to legible color combinations,

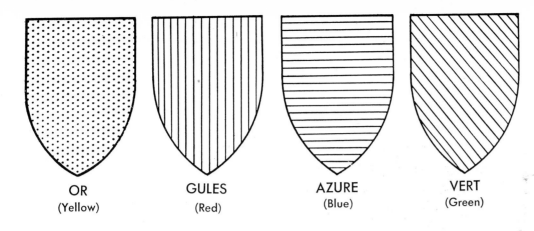

OR
(Yellow)

GULES
(Red)

AZURE
(Blue)

VERT
(Green)

Traditional heraldic desig-nations for color in black and white. This system has many convenient uses today.

black on yellow excels all others, followed by green on white, red on white, white on blue, black on white — combinations of red and green or red and blue being next to hopeless.

There is an important point to make in the isolation and diffusion of colors. Where opposite colors are employed in large area the effect may be bold and dramatic, although problems of apparent weight and dimension may be encountered. Yet where the same complements may be seen from a distance in small area or line and where they may be therefore confused or mixed by the eye, the stronger the contrast the weaker the result. Red and green may cancel each other completely. Adjacents which might lack vigor in large area may, when diffused, appear altogether brilliant and vibrant. These points should be borne in mind when color schemes for a building are to be seen from afar.

In the phenomenon of brightness contrast, dark colors tend to accent the brightness of light areas, and light grounds will add depth to deep colors. This illusion is illustrated.

The Element of Weight

Architects are — and should be — familiar with the quality of weight in color. Dark forms will rest uneasily and unhappily on light forms. Where structure and solidity are to be implied, deep colors serve best for the base and lighter colors for superstructures. Violation of this visual "law" is commonly seen. It emphasizes the need for keeping color integral with form and of building from the ground up with color just as the designer would with bulk.

To summarize, brightness will dominate darkness. Pure color will over-power gray color. Warm color will push cool colors into the background. Detail will command more notice and appear nearer than plainness.

ARGENT
(White or Silver)

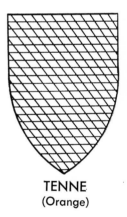

TENNE
(Orange)

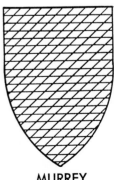

MURREY
(Red-Purple)

6

The Values
of Color

Unfortunately, not a great deal of reliable research has been conducted to measure the values of color. Although hearsay reports may be quoted by the score, these are likely to be exaggerated and to be influenced more by exuberance than by fact.

Because of the strong emotional appeal of color, individuals tend to have strong feelings about it, negative as well as positive. Where production records are involved, it is difficult to make allowance for added experience because of the time element. In the procedure of the author, notes are taken on production under existing conditions. After color has been introduced, no comparisons are made for at least two weeks. After this period, during which the worker accommodates his emotional attitude to the color effect, new sets of figures are assembled and the influence on production checked.

It is a known fact that human production-capacity will differ for many reasons. More work will be done in favorable weather than in bad, in summer than in winter, but less work will be done during excessive heat or cold. In studies of the effect of lighting, Luckiesh observed that, depending on mental attitude, production may increase even under conditions of extreme fatigue. In one experiment the performance of a difficult mechanical task reduced visual acuity 2 per cent and changed eye-muscle balance 5 per cent; yet the amount of work done increased 4 per cent. "Such a situation, in which *increasing production* takes place with *decreasing ability* to produce, forms a combination which is detrimental to the welfare of the worker and results in excessive fatigue and losses in nervous energy. It can be stated definitely that

Before and after views of business machine accounting office. In this study, supervised by the U.S. Public Health Service, better light and color was found to be worth $139.25 per worker per year.

Before and after views of accounting machines in U. S. Public Health Service study. Lighter color not only makes seeing easier but aids concentration by drawing attention to the task area.

the rate of working is not necessarily an indication of fatigue, since the results often indicate the opposite."

A decade ago the author, working with ophthalmologists, conducted many tests to determine what happened when human eyes were taxed. Poor light, glare, extreme contrast — all produced adverse effects. Now that the conditions for a proper working environment have been set — sufficient light of 30 footcandles or more for normal tasks, uniform brightness in the field of view — the need for tests no longer seems necessary. Technical study has established the requirements; industry merely needs to carry them out.

A General Survey

One of the most thorough investigations into the value of color in industry was published by the National Industrial Conference Board in 1947. Over 350 companies which had used color on a small or large scale were asked to comment in a long series of questions. The fact that a report was organized was in itself significant. Indeed the Board admitted a strong interest on the part of industry and acknowledged that more facts and case histories were needed.

It was found, however, that many "companies were unprepared to evaluate their programs primarily because of the difficulty involved in measuring the effects of a service as intangible as color." Yet despite the newness of the science of color conditioning, the facts divulged were quite impressive:

64.7 per cent of the companies stated that color had improved lighting.

27.9 per cent reported production increases.

30.9 per cent noted an improvement in the quality of work performed.

19.1 per cent commented favorably on reduced eyestrain and fatigue.

14.7 per cent credited color for reduced absenteeism.

All-in-all, 75 per cent of the companies were entirely or well satisfied with their color programs; 5.9 per cent were not satisfied; 19.1 per cent had no opinion one way or the other.

A Controlled Test

A competent and reliable evaluation of color has been prepared by the Public Buildings Service in Washington and the United States Public Health Service. This involved a two-year investigation of work production in a government office and was singular in that all details were carefully guided by authorities in the fields of vision, illumination, and color. Specifications for the use of color were prepared by the author. Production data were assembled by the Bureau of Internal Revenue.

A controlled study was undertaken to measure the working efficiency of a group of employees using business machines. Three conditions were analyzed: (1) the original room; (2) with the addition of new lighting fixtures; (3) with the further addition of color.

The fact that uniform brightness is essential to efficient and comfortable seeing has, from the medical standpoint, been confirmed by the above report. Under the first condition, the highest brightness in the room measured 1195; under the second condition it was 47, while under the third condition it was 20. Even more significant, brightness ratios under the first condition were over 100 to 1. The addition of new lighting reduced the ratio to 40 to 1 — still excessive. With proper color conditioning, the ratio was lowered to an ideal 4.7 to 1.

As to worker efficiency, one task had an improvement of 37.4 per cent. However, a conservative figure of 5.5 per cent was set as the general improvement shown in the department.

In cash value, this 5.5 per cent production improvement was equivalent to a saving on gross payroll of $13,229 among some 95 government employees. If this figure is a credible one — and the writer fully believes that it is — one may state that proper illumination and color are worth about $139.25 annually per average employee in American industry today! An organization having 100 employees would thus realize a year's saving of $13,925. For 1,000 employees the annual saving would be $139,250. These dollar figures, of course, would apply only where the before and after conditions were comparable to those of the government study. In the countless factories and offices that are as bad or worse, the dollar value of color is substantial and is hardly to be overlooked as a sound business investment.

Reduced Accident Frequencies

In the operation of a safety color code, to be described later, the United States Army Service Forces reported a reduction in accident frequencies in some government plants from a rate of 46.14 to 5.58. In one Quartermaster depot, disabling injuries were cut from 13.25 to 6.99.

Two very remarkable and complete records have been achieved with the author's aid in the shops of the New York City Transit System and the shore establishments of the U. S. Navy. In the first instance the program was preceded by an exhaustive study of facilities, equipment, machines, operations,

and accident hazards of all shops. Then, together with a supervisory training program and first aid courses for all employees, the Transit Board instituted a uniform color code defining hazards and emergency equipment throughout the shops, with statisticians alerted to follow the progress in accident prevention.

The colors used for the closely observed test had been checked scientifically to make allowance for the high frequency of color blindness (about 10 per cent) among men. The *vital* colors — yellow, orange, and blue — were put on the most dangerous spots; yellow for "strike-against," stumbling, and falling hazards, crane hooks, projections, car stanchions, and pit edges; orange for

A unified safety color code for the New York Board of Transportation reduced accidents over 40 per cent in a few months, for a saving of half a million dollars a year. Black and yellow were used to mark such hazards as shown here.

Gray on machinery, orange on cutting edges, blue on controls are further color standards applied by the New York Board of Transportation to curtail accidents.

the dangerous parts of cutting and forming devices, exposed rails, and wires; blue, as in the railroad industry, for marking equipment cut down for repair, and for switch boxes and controls in general to assure caution. Yellow, orange, and blue had been found to be readily distinguishable to even the average color-blind person. Green was used to mark first aid cabinets, stretchers, and gas masks. Red was used for fire protection equipment.

Hazards were marked in the specified paint colors by the workers themselves, with special union permission, so that the test had a definite starting time and a strong impact on personnel. Men familiar with special equipment and machines and with shop hazards became painters. Careful checking of the work assured consistency.

Not only was the program a marked long-term success, but its savings in injuries were immediate and impressive. Accidents in the Transit shops began to fall off at once, and 18 months after the introduction of the color code and safety program they had dropped 42.3 per cent.

In addition to its humanitarian aspects in fewer broken bones, sprains, and amputations, the Transit system's safety program paid a bonus far above its cost to management. Using generally accepted accident cost figures and applying them to the 38,000 employees of the New York City Transit System, the 42.3 per cent reduction in lost-time accidents is equivalent to an annual savings in excess of $500,000.

A similar and far more comprehensive record has been shown by the U. S. Navy. The same color code, developed by the author and included in a complete manual, has well proved its value. As reported by the Navy: "Indications are that the present manual has been used advantageously by the naval shore activities. It has been one of the contributing factors serving to reduce the Navy's industrial accident frequency rate from 6.4 in 1948 to 4.6 for 1951." Here the dollar value in reduced medical care and compensation would be approximately $1,300,000 in one year for civilian personnel (plus an equal or higher figure for enlisted personnel engaged in Navy industrial work).

Full credit for these records of safety improvement has not been claimed for the color markings on the various dangers alone, but these were the essential part of the program and the novel part. The colors are credited with serving a dual purpose in safety programs. They emphasize and delineate specific hazards, and their presence over-all is also thought by authorities to foster a greater degree of alertness and thus aid in the prevention of accidents.

School Children

Very important work in the school field with light and color has been conducted by D. B. Harmon of Texas. In making elaborate before-and-after studies of the influence of good light and color, he has shown significant results. Harmon is to be particularly congratulated on the thoroughness and fairness of his methods.

With higher light levels, a better control and distribution of light, brighter colors, a reorientation of desks, and better desks, he has done much to raise the standards of schoolhouse design and decoration.

Here are quotations from some of his findings. "In May, six months after the rooms had been redecorated and rearranged, the children were given the medical and nutritional examinations, and the visual, psychological, and education tests. At this time only 22.8 per cent of them showed refractive eye problems, a reduction of 57.1 per cent in the refractive eye problems found in the tests given to these children six months previously. . . . In addition, the nutrition problems had dropped to 39.5 per cent of the children, 44.5 per cent below the record for November, and the signs of chronic infection had been reduced 30.9 per cent below the record of six months previously. . . .

"In addition to the apparent improvements in physical well-being resulting from better use of natural light, some comparable results were obtained in educational achievement, as well. An objective achievement test measuring

educational growth in terms of months of educational age was given the children in the experimental building at the beginning and end of the six-month period. The same achievement test was given a comparable group of children in a comparable control building, but in which no lighting changes or room rearrangements were made.

"In the six-months' period of working in the rearranged classroom environments the children in the experimental school grew a mean average of 10.2 months in educational age, with a median growth of 10 months and a modal growth of 10 months. Seventy-six per cent of the children in the better lighted and optically consistent classrooms grew educationally over six months of educational age in the six-month interval. In the control school the mean educational growth was 6.8 months, the median six months, and the modal growth was six months. Only 33.4 per cent of the children in the control school grew educationally over six months of educational age."

Other Values

In industry, the functional application of color has now become more a coordinating task of top management. The executive approach is wise for two reasons. First, to see that color is put to intelligent purposes throughout the plant. Second, to make sure that any existing uses of it — by maintenance men, shop men, personnel men, safety supervisors — are not at cross purposes but reflect one consistent and unified direction.

Economies are many and may be summarized as follows:

Through color standardization, paint requirements may be reduced, costly inventories avoided, labor conserved.

A study of new materials may lead to greater durability and less need for maintenance.

Through good scientific practice, human productive capacity may be speeded up by relieving strain and tension, by making things easier to see and to operate with minimum fatigue.

Illumination may be improved. In some instances, the proper application of a coat of paint may actually obviate the need for more light.

Accident frequencies may be lowered at very substantial savings.

Better housekeeping, inspired by a practical and appealing use of color, may result in better machine maintenance, fewer rejects of manufactured products.

Morale may be strengthened — with attendant benefits in reduced absenteeism, lower labor turnover and cost of employee training.

7

Industrial Plants

and Office Buildings

This and the following chapter attempt to offer practical advice on the use of color in industrial and institutional fields. (Color in commercial establishments and homes will be the subject of the section on psychodécor.) General terms are used for the color designations, but the reader may turn to the spread following page 128, with its special chart of color chips, which contains samples that have been successfully used in the past.

Recommended Specifications

It is quite possible to set forth ideal brightness specifications for factory and office conditions. Ceilings — almost without exception — should be white. This will be essential to the efficiency of indirect lighting systems. In direct systems, the white overhead will reduce contrasts between fixtures and their surroundings. Being "neutral," white will also attract less psychological notice and hence prove non-distracting.

Upper walls (generally to a line level with the bottom of roof beams or trusses) should have a reflectance between 50 and 60 per cent if floors and equipment are on the dark side or between 60 and 70 per cent if most areas and surfaces in the interior are or can be made fairly light. Bright walls (above 70 per cent reflectance) seem to be allowable only where the most perfect and modern lighting system is installed and is accompanied by pale floors and equipment — or where critical seeing tasks are not performed, such as in storage rooms.

If a dado is required to conceal stains, the color tone should reflect not less than 25 per cent and perhaps not more than 40 per cent. Floors should reflect at least 25 per cent if such is practical. Machines, equipment, and desks should have a reflectance factor between 25 and 40 per cent, lighter when the floor is light and deeper when the floor is dark.

These ratios and percentages have been successfully applied in numerous plants and thus have the benefit of widespread trial and research.

Certain refinements are also to be introduced. Window sash ought to be white or a light tint (wall color) to lessen contrast with outside brightnesses. Machinery may be highlighted in accordance with the principles of Du Pont Three-Dimensional Seeing to reflect more light at important parts and concentrate the attention of the worker. In numerous fine seeing tasks, background shields may be constructed (a) to reflect light and provide immediate contrast with materials, (b) to confine the vision of the worker and hold eye adjustments relatively stable, (c) to blank off shadows or movement in the distance, and (d) to give the worker a better sense of isolation. Normally such shields should cover from 45 degrees to 60 degrees of the visual field but should be low enough to enable the worker to look about the room when he glances up.

End-wall treatments in medium tones also have widespread application. Where workers may be engaged at difficult eye tasks and may be so oriented as to face in the same direction, the wall ahead may be colored in a pleasing tint having a reflectance of from 25 to 40 per cent. The end wall will help to overcome an unfavorable constriction of the pupil. Upon looking up, it will afford relaxation rather than the stimulation of glare. It will likewise relax the strain of prolonged convergence and be psychologically pleasing and restful. Here again is a principle widely and successfully employed in industry.

Suitable Colors

For industrial purposes, soft, delicately grayish hues are best. They are lacking in aggression, are less distracting, and most effectively conceal dust and soiling. Ordinarily, primitive colors such as blue and yellow are tiresome. Where subtlety exists (bluish-green, peach, etc.) a more comfortable environment will be found, one that will "wear well" over prolonged periods.

It is logical to use "cool" colors such as green or blue where the working condition exposes the employee to relatively high temperatures. Conversely, "warm" tones of ivory, cream, or peach are suitable to soften up a vaulty or chilly space and compensate for lack of natural light.

One very practical color will be found in a soft tone of blue-green. Given a reflectance factor between 50 and 60 per cent, it has universal possibilities. It has an ideal brightness for average lighting conditions and will relieve glare as well as provide a neat sequence between light ceilings and average medium or deep tones on equipment and floors. Blue-green is a "cool" hue. It is not monotonous, having a bluish cast under daylight and a yellowish cast under artificial light. Best of all, it is the direct visual complement of human complexion. When the retina of the eye is saturated with it, a warm pinkish afterimage is produced which is flattering indeed to employees.

In working out color plans for industry, good colors (such as the above) and some amount of variety are recommended. Illumination and brightness should be supplemented by an intelligent consideration of color appeal.

In purely casual spaces, such as wash rooms, rest rooms, and cafeterias, lighter and cleaner hues may be used. In view of average color preferences, blue becomes ideal for facilities devoted to men, and rose for facilities devoted to women. In stairwells and corridors, usually deprived of natural light, bright tones of yellow are effective. In storage areas, white is best and will make the most of existing lighting installations.

The traditional use of gray and white in the U. S. Coast Guard has been supplemented by tones of green, yellow, and tan. Faber Birren, as color consultant, also devised a practical safety color code.

Critical Seeing Tasks

Where critical seeing tasks are performed, however, and where distractions are to be avoided, the best colors to use are soft variations of green, gray, and blue. Large, vaulty spaces may be enlivened with ivory, cream, or peach on all walls or yellow on end walls. Gray machinery highlighted with buff on important parts and working areas will prove effective. Medium gray is also ideal for unimportant elements such as bins, racks, shelving. One must remember that color is more compelling than neutrality. Hence, if it is strategically applied, it can bring order out of chaos, distinguish important from unimportant things, and help the worker in his mental effort to concentrate on his job. In theory as well as practice the purpose of color is not so much to "pep" up the worker; too much of this attitude may lead to distractions and irrelevancies. To the contrary, color becomes integral with the task, not foreign to it. Improved efficiency and relief from fatigue become automatic because the human eye can see more easily, with less strain. Color is made to fit in rather than stand out. It contributes to better visibility and to an agreeable and cheerful frame of mind.

Coordinated Programs

The author has had a wide fund of experience in the color coordination of large building projects, new and old. Automotive plants, steel mills, textile mills, breweries, food processing plants, chemical industries have all been surveyed and specifications written. While different problems are to be encountered, there are many similar elements.

In forge shops and foundries, for example, painting is not always practical. It may be wise to confine color to small work spaces — if not to walls and overhead — to aid seeing and identity.

The old tradition of choosing colors to accommodate orientation — cool colors for south and west exposures, warm colors for north and east exposures — seldom applies to industrial conditions. Here it is far more important to relate color to task, to use bright luminous hues for large, vaulty spaces, grayish colors to avoid distractions in critical seeing tasks, fairly rich and emotionally compelling colors in rest rooms, wash rooms, and cafeterias.

Recently two comprehensive jobs of color coordination were completed for the U. S. Navy and Coast Guard. The first of these involved all so-called shore establishments — ship yards, ordnance plants, air stations, barracks, administrative and personnel quarters, hospitals, recreation areas — as well

Color standardization in the U. S. Coast Guard has been extended to the exteriors of vessels. The photo at the right shows a cutter after repainting.

as all transportation equipment — shore facilities, cranes, derricks, etc.

The entire Navy assignment necessitated only 26 color standards, including those set aside for purposes of a safety code. (In average large industries about 16 colors are required for all purposes.)

There were three standard grays for machinery, a medium tone being used for average equipment, a light tone for precision instruments, and a deep tone for large, bulky machines such as cutting and forming presses.

The medium gray was also used for most automotive equipment.

Exterior colors were limited to two grays, white, and buff — with the same standards for trim.

In interior treatments, one uniform gray on trim, doors, door frames, and radiators obviated the need for a deeper harmonizing tone for each separate wall tone, ivory, green, gray, yellow, peach, blue. This lent real efficiency to the cost of painting and kept the color inventory at a minimum.

For industrial interiors, medium gray was used for dado, with yellow on upper walls. In interiors where green was used, the dado for average facilities had a medium tone and a deep green dado was specified for heavy operations. A series of bright colors for safety were employed also for piping identification, compressed gas cylinders, and the like.

The United States Coast Guard has developed a paint and color manual to effect simplification and to coordinate its extensive facilities. Faber Birren served as consultant. The plan is simple, in order to permit efficient maintenance by, in many instances, inexperienced personnel. Photos show a typical barracks and amateur painters at work.

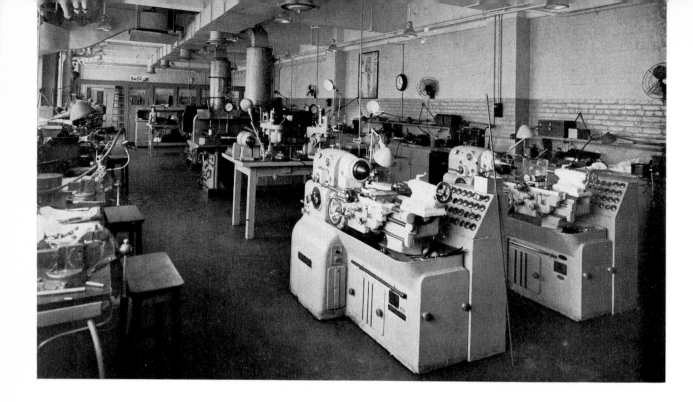

One of the most comprehensive programs of color coordination is that of the U. S. Navy, developed with the assistance of Faber Birren. Only twenty-six standards, including a unified color code for safety, are used for the extensive facilities of the Navy: all its shore structures, machinery, and equipment. Photo shows machine shop in which conditions have been made most efficient by the correct application of color.

In the second program, for the Coast Guard, the above Navy standards and practices were adopted in substantial part. In addition, color applications were written for vessels, aircraft, and miscellaneous facilities individual to Coast Guard operations, such as light stations, buoys, rescue equipment. This report included further data on paints, coating systems, and surface preparation. The complete manual (which well serves as a model for industry) assures savings by (a) standardization and simplification, (b) reduced paint inventories, (c) better technical practice in the use of paint finishes, (d) better scientific practice in the use of color for improved efficiency, and (e) a promise of reduced accident frequencies, medical costs, and compensation because of emphasis on safety.

In similar but smaller programs for office buildings, like practices have been successfully employed.

For example, a uniform light gray for walls and a uniform medium gray for trim may be carried on all outer peripheral walls and on metal partitions. Inner walls may then be peach, green, yellow as desired. Not only may functions be served, but the cost of painting (about three-quarters for labor and one-quarter for materials) may be held to a minimum.

Too frequently the color program, when not well organized, comprises a series of individual efforts and exceptions. Literally dozens and hundreds of tones may be used extravagantly and needlessly. Emotionally considered, colors may be endless. Functionally, however, good scientific practice will require but a few.

Safety

The protection of human life and limb is to be well achieved through the aid of color. Though many accidents may be caused through inexperience and pressure for more output, a meaningful use of color can serve remarkable ends. If seeing is poor, the worker may be exposed to a number of hazards.

With insufficient visibility, the dangers of his task may automatically mount.

In his effort to carry out his assignments his entire body may be strained.

Glare, dimness, and poor contrast may have deleterious effects in the severe dilation of his pupil during the course of the day.

Being nervous, fatigued, and with his eyes far below par in acuity, he naturally risks accident. His work may fall off in quality, and the general resistance of his body may be lowered.

The well ordered plant has bright, colorful walls, medium tones on equipment, machinery and floors, with hazards clearly defined in accordance with a unified safety code. (Dana B. Merrill photograph.)

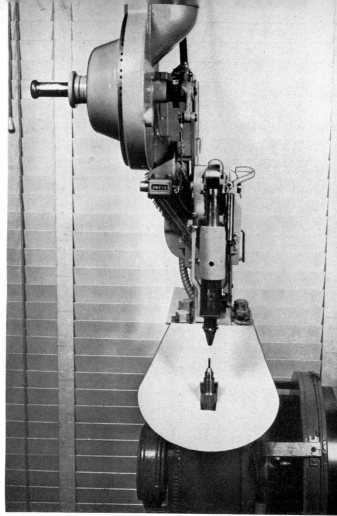

Good safety practice as applied to a riveting machine. Light color, with a special shield back of the vital point, aids visibility, increases safety, and removes distractions for greater speed and fewer accidents. (J. Walker Grimm photographs.)

To relieve all this, light and color may be intelligently engineered. Human beings have the remarkable capacity of concentrating effort under adverse situations through sheer power of application. One can read a telephone directory in the dim environs of a telephone booth, run that last hundred feet to a departing train, drive that last mile home at three in the morning. But these are not the conditions under which tasks are best accomplished.

Yet in industries throughout the country men and women labor at tasks in every way as trying as the reading of six-point type in a dark booth. They "drive that last mile home" as they struggle to operate a machine at the end of an eight-hour day. Management, in a casual way, may too often look for two minutes at an operation and, not finding it severe, fail to understand why someone else can't look at it all day. And because human eyes will stand up under great abuse, the worker himself may be fooled. He may not recognize that his fatigue, nausea, headache, may trace back to hours spent endeavoring to see that which was not adequately visible. He may blame a cut finger or a broken limb on his own carelessness and not on his eyes.

An Organized Code

Increased levels of illumination have in many instances improved industrial efficiency and reduced the frequency of accidents. In one instance, raising the average illumination from 2 to 19 footcandles lowered the accident-frequency rate 54 per cent. In another plant raising the average illumination from 8 to 30 footcandles reduced accidents 11 per cent. A British investigation in the printing industry showed that the efficiency of the night staff went up 33 per cent when the footcandle level was raised to 20-25 footcandles.

As to color, a unified code was organized by the author during 1942-43. This was presented at a convention of the National Safety Council in 1943 and issued in complete form by Du Pont in February of 1944. Subsequently, at the request of the U. S. Government the code was adopted in substantial part by the American Standards Association.

The features of the code are as follows:

Machine shop, New York Trade School. Du Pont, General Electric, and Faber Birren cooperated in the design of a functional working environment. Note general uniformity of brightness to make seeing easy and comfortable.

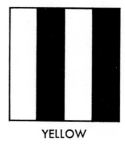

YELLOW

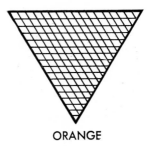

ORANGE

GREEN

Yellow (or yellow and black bands) is standard to mark strike-against, stumbling, or falling hazards. It is painted on obstructions, low beams, dead ends, the edges of platforms and pits. Being the color of highest visibility in the spectrum it is conspicuous under all lighting conditions and well adapted to the above purposes. The Navy also uses black and yellow in the form of a checkerboard to mark eye-hazardous areas, such as in arc welding. It is painted on welding shields, signs, and equipment to guard against flash burns of the eye.

Orange (symbolized by a triangle) is standard for acute hazards likely to cut, crush, burn, or shock the worker. It is painted around the edges of cutting machines and rollers. On the inside areas of machine guards and electric switch boxes, it "shouts loudly" when such devices are removed or left open.

Green (symbolized by a cross) is standard to identify first aid equipment, cabinets for stretchers, gas masks, medicines, and the like.

Red (symbolized by a square) is reserved entirely and exclusively for the marking of fire protection devices. It is painted on walls back of extinguishers, on floors to prevent obstruction, on valves and fittings for hose connections.

Blue (symbolized by a circle) is standard as a caution signal. The railroad industry employs it to mark cars which should not be moved. In factories it is placed as a symbol on equipment, elevators, machines, tanks, ovens, etc., cut down for repair. It may be used on switch control boxes as a silent and unobtrusive reminder for the worker to see that his machine is clear before he operates it.

A new symbol, comprised of a purple target on yellow, has recently been established to mark dangerous radioactive materials and radiochemicals. It is used on doors, containers, labels, and the like to warn and instruct against exposure.

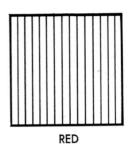

RED

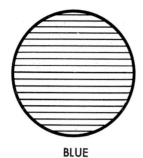

BLUE

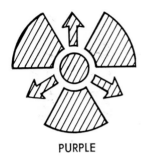

PURPLE

Safety color code. In a nationally accepted color code for safety, colors and symbols are combined to mark hazards: black and yellow (stripes) for strike-against, falling, stumbling, obstructions; orange (triangle) for acute hazards, sharp edges, rollers, gears; green (cross) to identify first aid equipment; red (square) to mark fire protection devices; blue (disk) for switch boxes, electrical controls, and equipment cut down for repair; purple (target) to distinguish the hazards of radioactive materials and radiochemicals.

View of Isotope and Semi-Works Building at Oak Ridge National Laboratory. Light colors on ceiling, wall, and floors make for clear visibility. Courtesy of The Austin Company.

In its Certified Office Planning Service, the Wood Office Furniture Institute offers decorative aid to office managers. The program, worked out with the assistance of Faber Birren, coordinates standard wood finishes with carpeting, resilient floor coverings, paints, textiles, upholstery materials. (James R. Dunlop photograph.)

White, gray, and black are standard for traffic control and good housekeeping. They are used for aisle marks and are painted on waste receptacles. White corners and baseboards may be used to discourage littering and to get the sweeper to dig into corners.

The safety code colors may also be employed for piping identification. According to specifications set up by the American Standards Association (A13-1928), red may be used for fire protection; yellow and orange for dangerous materials; green, white, black, and gray for safe materials; blue for protective materials; and purple for extra valuable materials.

Heat Reflection

The technique of color in the control of temperature is very simple. White and all light colors repel heat through reflection; black and all dark colors absorb it.

Conference room, Reinhold Publishing Corporation, New York. Blue and green in light and dark tones create a restful and non-distracting environment. (Ben Schnall photograph.)

The U. S. Bureau of Mines has given some important facts on heat absorption and reflection as they affect evaporation in gasoline storage tanks of 12,000 gallon capacity. Over a period of $4\frac{1}{2}$ months, a tank painted white and having an insulated housing had an evaporation loss of 112 gallons, or 1.40 per cent. A tank covered with aluminum foil had a loss of 170 gallons, or 2.12 per cent. A tank with aluminum paint had a loss of 187 gallons, or 2.34 per cent. A red tank had a loss of 284 gallons, or 3.54 per cent.

President's office, Reinhold Publishing Corporation, New York. An excellent example of color variety. Walls are in blue and off-white, rug in gold, draperies in natural linen, chair upholstery in blue. Even the painting is in harmony. (Ben Schnall photograph.)

Reception room, Reinhold Publishing Corporation, New York. There is sprightly interest — and complete relief from monotony — in the use of walnut panels, white ceiling, black floor, blue end-wall, with upholstery in blue and orange. (Ben Schnall photograph.)

The difference of 114 gallons between white and red (and it would be
larger still between white and black) would be serious in any sizable tank
field. White, even though it cost more, would be economical.

More conservative facts on the efficiency of white in heat reflection are
given by the Du Pont Company in a folder devoted to its Dulux White for
Tanks. Here a saving of $\frac{1}{3}$ per cent is mentioned, "in comparison with
previous practical finishes." In quoting one case history, the average maximum temperature for a tank painted with Dulux white was 63.1° over
a period of several months. In other tanks the average maximum temperature was 70.1°.

As to home radiators, aluminum and gold paints have long been thought

A reception area in the offices of Container Corporation of America. The offices were designed and color specified by the Department of Design of Container Corporation of America. Color plate courtesy of *Scope*.

Reception area, Cambridge Tile Manufacturing Co., Cincinnati. Soft grays, offset by muted tones of coral, green, and yellow, give majesty to one of the most beautiful and durable of all building materials — ceramic tile. (Lodder photograph.)

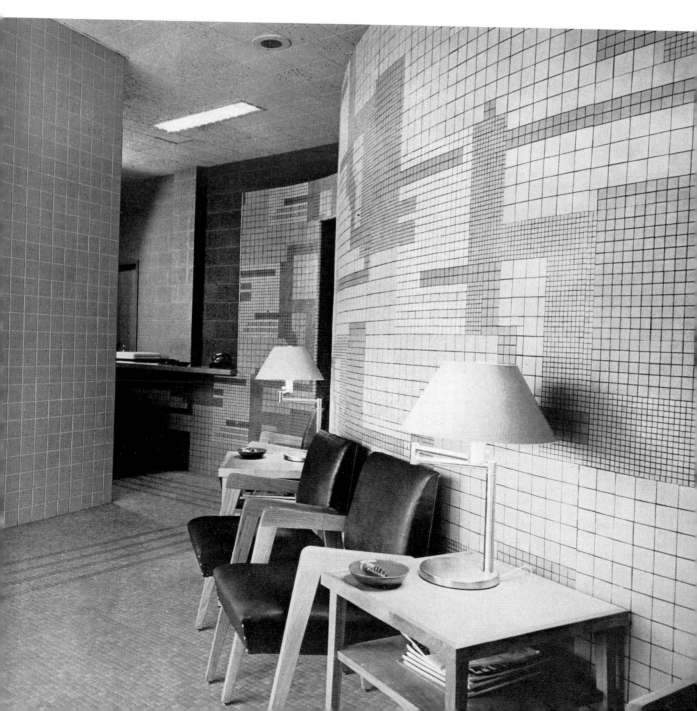

most efficient. The fact, however, is that metallic paints reduce heat transmission and are not as desirable as other types. In a circular issued by the U. S. Bureau of Standards the following data are quoted: "The effect of adding metallic paint is equivalent to removing $\frac{1}{6}$ of the radiator or nearly 17 per cent. Or as if one section out of six had been removed. Thus a radiator of five sections painted with white or a light color should be about as efficient as another of six sections painted with metallic paint."

Many other examples are to be described. Aluminum foil makes an excellent insulating baffle in buildings, ships, airplanes and equipment such as refrigerators. The hold of a white ship in the tropics will be at least 10 degrees cooler than the hold of a black ship. A Texas bus system found that a white top lowered summer temperatures by 10 to 15 per cent. An airline

Reception area in Herman Miller New York showroom. Ceiling and floor are dark, to concentrate attention at the desk. Courtesy of Alfred Auerbach Associates.

found a difference of some 28 degrees between an unpainted aluminum cabin and one in which white paint had been applied to the top area only. This difference, of course, was noted on a hot, sunny day.

In a study of shop helmets the U. S. Navy reorganized its identification code after finding a difference of 22 degrees (inside the crown) between a white and a black helmet on a sunny day.

Insect Repellents

Finally a mention of color as an insect repellent. By and large most insects are blind to red radiation but are able to respond to ultraviolet. Thus with light sources, red and orange lamps of low wattage will hold less attraction

Herman Miller showroom, New York. Yellow and purple panels are suspended from a black ceiling. All emphasis is on the furniture displayed. Courtesy of Alfred Auerbach Associates.

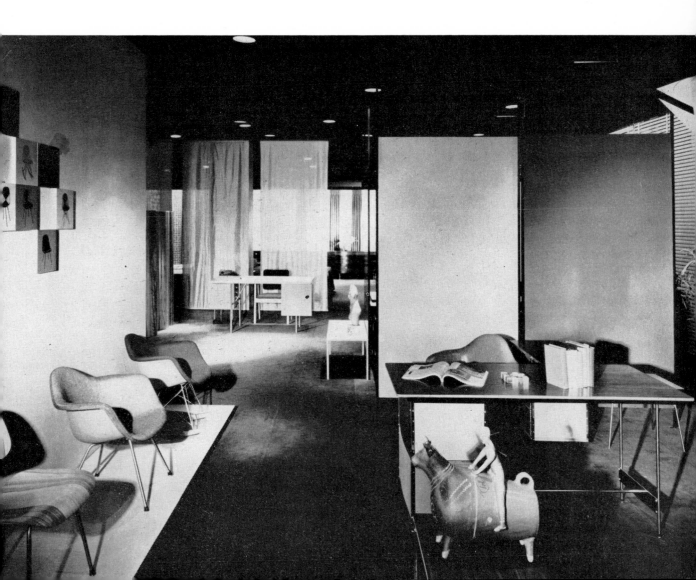

View of general offices, Container Corporation of America, Chicago. One of the first examples — and still one of the best — of the modern, functional use of color in office decoration. With warm gray as a sequence color, varied tones are used over end walls. Brighter hues are applied to corridors and reception rooms, less distracting tones to working areas. The variety is great, yet the plan "hangs together" perfectly because of expert control.

than higher intensity lamps and radiation sources emitting energy in the blue and ultraviolet region of the electromagnetic spectrum. Both may be effectively employed at the same time to repel indirectly and attract directly.

For house flies, contradictory results have been reported. The safest conclusion is that flies are more attracted to lightness than to darkness. In Holland horse stables and cow barns are frequently painted with pale blue in the hope of ridding them of pests. However, the representative of a large Dutch paint company reports that this use of blue is supported more by superstition than by fact.

Regarding mosquitoes, however, there is better agreement. Here light colors are the repelling ones. When boxes are lined with navy blue, pink, gray and yellow flannel, the interiors of the blue and gray boxes have been found to harbor the most insects, whereas the pink and yellow boxes have been relatively free of mosquitoes.

8

Schools and

Hospitals

Color has vital bearing on health and human welfare. The remarkable work of D. B. Harmon in the school field has well demonstrated that glare and faulty light distribution can affect posture, fatigue, health, mental capacity. According to Harmon, "We are prone because of our cultural or mentalistic points of view, to think of seeing as being independent of all other processes set into action by the eye — but, when light stimulates the eye, many bodily processes are set into action to keep the body's mechanics and chemistry in balance, in spite of our cultural emphasis on only one of them."

Control of Daylight

Numerous developments have appeared in recent years bearing on the control of daylight. Light-directional glass block, for example, will refract light in an upward direction, throw it diffusely over ceilings and upper walls and cut down the direct glare of sunlight.

For traditional types of schoolrooms having tall windows, Harmon has devised special light diffusers. These are placed at an angle the full length of the window wall to scatter direct sunlight. The lower part of the window is left clear as a "vision strip."

Daylight, of course, is the condition under which human eyes have developed. In schools particularly, control of natural light is economically wise and desirable. Because of color constancy, vision is effectively conducted

under widely different intensities of light. Those who are concerned about the instability of natural light (during the day) must not forget that shifts in illumination not only are capably handled by the eye, but they produce a certain comfort and lack of monotony. With the human body, in a constant state of flux, unvarying sensations are perhaps more tiring than shifting and changing ones.

Daylight control may be advantageously regulated through the use of

A rehabilitated school room in which light-directional glass block has replaced conventional windows. Note improved lighting and effective use of paint. Courtesy of Owens-Illinois Glass Co.

Comparative views of same classroom: with uncovered windows, with fully shaded windows, and with Venetian blinds. While conventional opaque shades do little more than blot out light, Venetian blinds will not only remove window glare but improve lighting on the far side of the room as much as 30 per cent as compared with full window openings. Courtesy of Hunter Douglas Corporation.

Venetian blinds (see illustrations). In experiments conducted for the Hunter Douglas Corporation, excellent light distribution has been achieved which, instead of blocking out sunlight, has made use of it. In many schools the strange practice of blotting out light on sunny days is paradoxical indeed. Sunlight should obviously be utilized, and the Venetian blind is one good device to employ.

In actual tests, Venetian blinds have been found to increase light levels at the far side of a room as much as 34 per cent — as against full window openings. This is readily explained by the fact that direct rays of sunlight may enter a window, hit the floor and be absorbed. The Venetian blind not only will convert these directional rays into softly diffused light — scattering it throughout an interior — but will smooth out high brightness differences (glare). In other words, sunlight will be put to use rather than wasted. Brightness ratios of 100 to 1 or more may at the same time be reduced to less than 5 to 1 for efficient and comfortable seeing.

At night as well, the Venetian blind can accomplish the further purpose of reflecting artificial light back into a room rather than permitting it to be wasted through glass windows or glass block. Light level at the window may be increased some 10 per cent. In addition, relatively uniform brightness between walls and window openings can be maintained to agree with good scientific practice.

 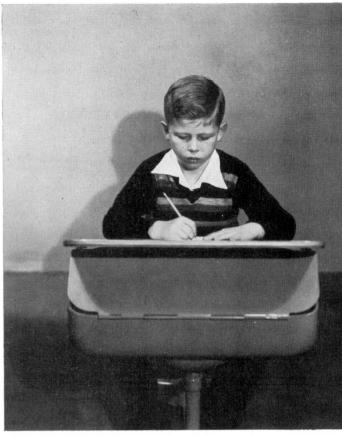

Problems in Schools

Today, nearly 60 per cent of school children have eye defects. The percentage may run from 18 in the first grade to more than 80 at the end of the elementary period. About 30 per cent of average pupils have posture disturbances which can be attributed, in part at least, to abuse of the eyes and to physical efforts to see clearly. Backward children are also notoriously subject to various eye defects.

D. B. Harmon has written, "Organisms, including man, do not see to see — they see to act." Hence, it is not enough to use pretty colors in the school environment. A far greater duty is to make sure that the seeing task is made relatively simple, that illumination and brightness are well balanced, and that minimum effort is required for the pupil to coordinate visual and physical reactions.

There is a trend today toward the use of pale and light colors, approaching white. While such tints may be efficient in reflecting light, they are not always best and easiest on the eyes. M. Luckiesh writes, "In general, it may be concluded that a brighter surrounding field is more detrimental than a darker one . . . . Visual efficiency is at a maximum when the brightness of the central field is equal to that of the surroundings . . . . A brighter surrounding field reduces visual efficiency more than one which is darker than the central field."

In the writing of color specifications for schools, it is easy to describe and explain the general principles and technical factors that should be considered. To begin with, color in and of itself may be of less importance than the quality of brightness. It is brightness that reflects the light, regulates the eye, aids or defeats visibility.

Yet all colors are meaningless without light. In the illumination of schoolrooms, lighting should be adequate (30 footcandles or more). And equally important, such illumination should be as evenly distributed as possible. When daylight is used, desks adjacent to windows may receive many times more light than desks at the far side of the room. Venetian blinds, as already described, high transmittance shades, and horizontally or vertically louvered blinds may be needed to deflect and scatter the direct rays of the sun.

When artificial light sources are employed, again a fairly uniform distribution of light is wanted. Exposed lamp bulbs or fluorescent tubes are inimical to good seeing, particularly where the ceiling is low. In many respects the semi-indirect system is excellent. Here the lamps or tubes are covered by semi-opaque diffusers or are hidden by baffles. Because light is reflected from the ceiling and also transmitted from the fixture, the eye is not troubled by great brightness extremes. Where the lighting system is well designed, the ceiling brightness approximately equals the fixture brightness, the entire overhead being soft and luminous.

Suggested Reflectances

To achieve maximum efficiency from natural and artificial light sources, the ceiling, in practically all cases, should be white. This is advantageous where window diffusers or Venetian blinds are installed and where indirect or semi-indirect fixtures are used. Colors on ceilings distract attention and waste light. To make ceilings anything but white is equivalent to cutting down the intensity of illumination as though by a rheostat. Obviously, the schoolroom needs more light, not less.

As to walls, normally there is seldom need for paints that reflect more than 60 per cent of light. With reflectances higher than this, serious trouble may be encountered. Conditions of excessive glare may be introduced and the eye may be handicapped rather than aided.

Attention should also, of course, be paid to the floor and to equipment. Natural woods, when kept clean, reflect about 25 per cent of light. With a 50-60 per cent tone used on walls, and white on the ceiling which is generally out of direct range of vision, the student may look about the room without discomfort. His eye can stay at one steady adjustment. Because eyestrain has muscular origin, fatigue, nervousness, and tension will be reduced.

As to appearance, the average human complexion also reflects about 50 per cent of light. Hence, there will be no unfavorable contrast with walls, no bright areas that may cause "blur" and "halos" when the pupils look at one another or at the instructor.

Thus it is practical to have white for the ceiling; 50 to 60 per cent reflectance for the walls; 25 per cent or better reflectance for floors and equipment.

Color Schemes

With the best principles of brightness engineering applied, the more psychological quality of color may be considered. Choice here may also follow a technical method and capitalize a wealth of research.

In general, such colors as ivory and pale yellow are excellent for corridors, stairwells, and rooms deprived of natural light but not used for critical seeing tasks. These colors suggest sunlight, add apparent luminosity to existing light sources, and offer an interesting sequence with other and more subdued tones recommended for classrooms.

In the classroom itself, a number of colors and color effects are appropriate. In the main, the two best hues to employ are a pale blue-green and a peach. Pale yellows and blues, being primitive in quality, are likely to appear rather bleak and monotonous.

Tones such as ivory, buff, and tan lack character and are more or less associated with the conventions of the past. However, peach (a combination of yellow and orange with white) and blue-green (a combination of blue and green with white) have subtlety and beauty and are suitable for rooms occupied for long periods of time.

Peach as a classroom color may be specified for elementary grades and for rooms having north exposure or where natural light may be weak, such as in courts. Blue-green is excellent for secondary grades, for study areas, and for rooms having south exposure.

Colors on End Walls

If wall colors should have a reflectance of from 50 to 60 per cent, the treatment of end walls should also be considered. Because students are generally seated so as to face in one direction, there is an opportunity to treat the front end of the room in a slightly softer and deeper tone having a reflectance of from 25 to 40 per cent. Such areas will serve a number of functional purposes.

They will provide visual and emotional relaxation. They will rest the eyes and allow for better visibility. The appearance of the instructor and the exhibition of any charts or materials will be improved, simply because it is easier for the eye to see lightness against darkness than darkness against lightness. In brief, the whole process of vision is one that reacts quickly to light objects and surfaces and slowly to dark ones. Where the end wall treatment is applied as suggested, the best in seeing efficiency and comfort is assured.

Good colors to use for end walls are medium blue-greens, soft grayish blues, deep peach, or rose tones. These may be variously handled. The medium blue-green end wall may have pale blue-green sidewalls, or peach sidewalls where a more vigorous effect is wanted. The deep peach or rose end wall may be used with warm tones on the sidewalls, or complementary tints, such as pale green or blue. One impressive device is to color the side and rear walls in a light pearl gray. This tone, being neutral, will lend itself to almost any end wall treatment.

Where there are blackboards it is preferable to have them surrounded by medium tones rather than light ones, to reduce contrast and minimize visual shock. Current developments will undoubtedly lead to the replacement of conventional blackboards with materials of lighter tone. This will be a great improvement for it will mean greater lighting efficiency and will make possible the use of generally lighter colors in the classroom.

Regarding the blackboard itself, Harmon has reached a number of unconventional conclusions after extensive and competent research. Visibility, for example, is by no means the sole criterion simply because "momentary recognition can be under a high degree of stress which would defeat the performance of a sustained, visually-centered task." In other words, sharp black and white contrast, while unquestionably easy to see, may at the same time cause discomfort when fixated over long periods.

Harmon concludes that (a) greatest disadvantage lies in a dark chalk on a light board; (b) dark green boards hold no particular merit over black boards; (c) yellow chalk on a light green board (having about 20 per cent reflectance) is just about right. The writer would add that the reflectance (20 per cent) is probably the important factor, not so much the green hue. Simply, moderate contrast between board and chalk is desirable for what Harmon terms sustained vision. Extremely high contrast and visibility belong more to outdoor signs than to indoor school workboards.

The Hospital

Color for the sake of color is hardly enough to answer the needs of hospitals. Although admittedly it is better than drabness or the excessive "sterility" of white, it requires some conservatism and purpose in its use.

The very nature of hospital service would suggest that every application of color be technically correct, that matters of appearance be supplemented, if not dominated in those areas where patients are, by a vital regard for visual and physical comfort above mere esthetic pleasure.

While almost any hue may be considered attractive, not all colors or tones of color have equal utility and value. Choice and discrimination should be founded on reason and function, and a set of hospital specifications may be written that adhere to good scientific practice.

With such an attitude in mind, intelligent order and purpose can be put into the design of a hospital color plan, brilliant in some locations, reserved in others.

In lobbies, reception rooms, parlors, and solaria variety should be introduced. These spaces normally are frequented by visitors as well as patients. Too much of any color should be avoided. There is a psychological reason for this. All-over color effects invite definite emotional reactions which may be unfavorable as well as favorable.

To shift emphasis from any precise mood, neatly chosen color sequences will help to break up monotony and treat the eye to an interesting "change of pace." Pale ivory or peach walls, for example, may be contrasted against soft tones of green or blue in floors, draperies, upholstered furniture. Or soft green or blue on walls may be accompanied by rose tones in furnishings. Also, it is often desirable to carry out the warm effect in enclosed spaces deprived of natural light and to use the cool hues for adjoining rooms.

If, as the patient or visitor walks about, he is exposed alternately to warm and cool effects, severity will be avoided and any feeling of excitation or depression will be relieved because of variety rather than uniformity. This is a psychological device that has universal appeal and may be used with excellent success where relatively large groups of people are involved.

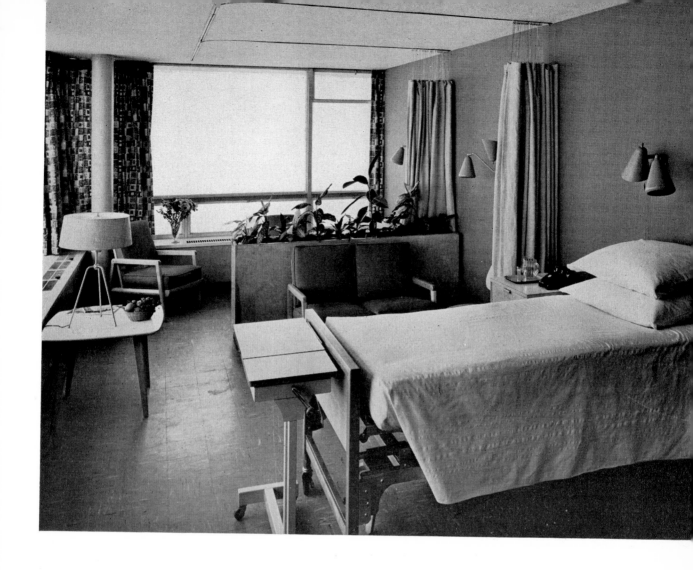

General Hospital Areas

In corridors and stairways, the use of color may be planned to compensate for lack of natural light. Pale yellow and peach are ideal. They not only appear "sunny" but are moderately aggressive in quality; they "pick up" the mood and provide agreeable contrast with softer and cooler tones recommended for private rooms and wards.

In accommodations devoted to patients, good color practice would suggest the following principles. First of all, wall tones should be a trifle grayish and not too bright. Such "muted" colors (with a reflectance of from 50 to 60 per cent) will be restful, free of impulsive distraction, and practical in resisting soiling and abuse.

Ceilings may be in a lighter tint of the wall hue. While it might be desirable to use soft tones of peach, rose, and ivory for north exposures and soft tones of

Varied pastel colors give light and cheer to this deluxe room in the Lankenau Hospital in Overbrook, Pennsylvania. Vincent G. Kling, architect. (Lawrence S. Williams photograph.)

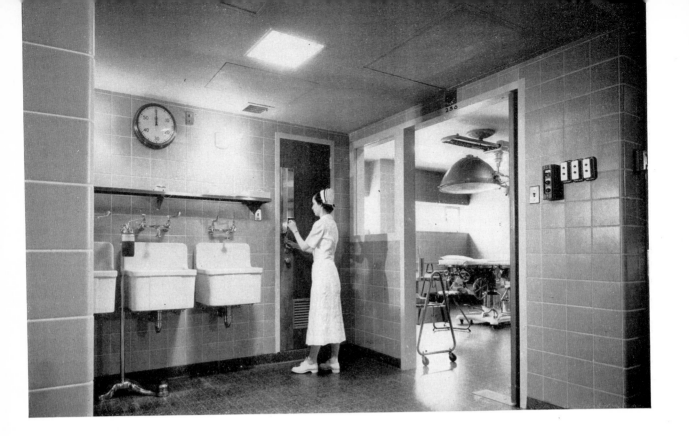

Operating suite, Edward John Noble Hospital, Gouverneur, New York. Skidmore, Owings & Merrill, architects. Soft green tile walls relieve glare and complement the hue of human blood and tissue — an aid to surgery. (Torkel Korling photograph.)

green, blue, and gray for south exposures, a better principle is to try to restrict the warmer hues for convalescent patients and the cooler hues for chronic patients. Rooms may also be "conditioned" through regulation of illumination, dim levels of light being restful and brighter light more stimulating.

Hospital Color Schemes

Three major color effects are proposed. The first of these is a soft blue-green, the complement of human complexion. This color creates a cool and relaxing environment.

The second scheme is comprised of a soft peach, the tint of human complexion itself. In relatively small interiors (without much sunlight) it tends to increase room dimensions.

The third scheme is to use a soft pearl gray, relieved by delicate multi-colors in furniture, flooring, and draperies. Gray is a beautiful and functional color when it is agreeably harmonized. It is, of course, a perfect foil for almost all other hues.

In operating rooms and surgical departments, blue-green is also suitable. Large expanses of white, regardless of their apparent cleanliness, are trying

A

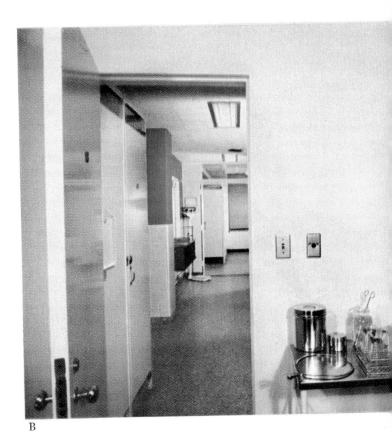

B

Chicago Lying-in Hospital of the University of Chicago Clinic. Semi-private room (A), a corridor in the outpatient department (B), and a climate room (C). The redecorating project was carried out under the direction of Mrs. Walter P. Paepcke, Chairman of the House Committee of the Women's Board, with the supervisory help of Walter C. Granville, Assistant Director, Department of Design, Container Corporation of America. Courtesy of *Scope*.

C

on vision. They constrict the pupil of the eye and make seeing difficult.

Nurses' stations may be in pale yellow or peach for a slightly aggressive effect. Utility rooms, diet kitchens, and linen rooms may be white where occupancy is not too constant. Otherwise, pale green or blue-green is advised.

Where patients or staff may be exposed to relatively high temperatures, such as physical therapy, x-ray rooms, and laundry, blue-green is ideal. In offices and laboratories, however, the color effect may be guided by room orientation — ivory for north and east exposures, gray or green for south and west exposures.

Blue as a color should generally be avoided over large areas. It has a depressing effect on many persons and seems to trouble the eye by causing a nearsighted adjustment of the lens. However, it holds universal popularity and makes an excellent choice for occasional end walls, floors, upholstery fabrics, and incidental accessories.

Other Facilities

In classrooms and conference rooms, end wall treatments may be employed. Here the device is to use a light color, such as ivory, on the side and back walls of the room for high light reflection, and to paint the end wall faced by the students in a medium tone of green or blue. This will cut down glare, relieve the eyes, and build up higher visibility for the doctor or instructor or for any charts or demonstrations presented.

End walls in soft colors have many applications. Dark, vaulty spaces may be enlivened with an end wall in yellow. In laboratories where critical seeing tasks are performed, deeper hues on end walls will give the eye a chance to rest and will provide convenient areas for visual and emotional relaxation.

For dispensaries, light pearl gray is ideal for the waiting room, relieved by furnishings in cheerful red or blue, or a combination of both. Examining and treatment rooms may be in blue-green. Dressing rooms and toilets may be in peach to reflect a healthful glow upon the flesh.

In the nurses' home, more of an interior designer's point of view may be expressed. However, here again research in color preference may be relied upon to make sure that each use of color has unquestioned appeal. Rose tones hold great popularity among women and hence are ideal for parlors and bedrooms. In dining rooms, studies in the psychological associations existing between colors and foods have shown peach to be the most "appetizing" of all hues. It affords an appropriate and pleasing environment and is harmoniously relieved by the use of blue in draperies and furnishings.

California residence of Charles Eames. Here, color and modern architecture are at their freshest and newest. Insert panels are in a striking variety of hues. (Charles Eames photograph.)

9

Building Exteriors

Color on building exteriors is a debatable subject. Different schools of thought, some tolerant, some not, have different viewpoints. Some with classical taste fail to recognize that their modern Greek and Roman forms contradict the expression of ancient times, when most sculpture and the façades of temples were hued.

By training, the architect is a man more sensitive to form than to color, and perhaps rightly so. Design and construction are difficult problems; color selection is relatively easy. Yet in the final result, as frequently happens, the color is what may strike the public eye and stimulate the greater emotional response.

Whether the exterior of buildings should be colored or not is less important, in the author's opinion, than consideration of design and architectural style. Color looks wonderful in some instances and terrible in others. Region and locale, an urban setting or a rural one, the spirit which a building should convey (a church, for example, as against a theater), all these should influence any decisions.

Color Is Integral with Form

Were an architect to conceive his forms with the broad side of colored chalk or pastel rather than to outline them with the sharp point of a pencil, the importance of color-mass might be more evident. Quite commonly the whole conception of a building is visualized with pencil lines, and the whole beauty of it portrayed in terms of lines and shapes. This may be one reason why gray stone is a preferred building material, for it seems to negate the factor of color. Yet no form is possible without color, gray to the contrary. And gray in the emotional sense is austere, cold, solemn. Gothic architecture is perhaps gray architecture, what with its play of light and shadow. But gray limestone does not lend itself to other and more blithe moods. The attempt to give design and form buoyant action is next to impossible where the material used is ashen in tone.

Textile Building at 1407 Broadway, New York. The exterior is green ceramic brick, a color that complements the massive simplicity of the architecture. Kahn & Jacobs, architects. (Michael Miller photograph.)

Metropolitan Architecture

A person has good reason to wonder if the American spirit is gray. Should capitols and public buildings be gray? Should classical forms — which originally were hued — be sapped of color?

In the large American cities, gray stone and brick predominate in tall commercial buildings. Although the decentralization of population is philosophically recommended in the architectural press, the big cities get bigger and more crowded, and the farms grow even more sparse. Apparently Americans like to live together. Decentralization holds little charm for them.

As cities expand, the need for color increases. And as civilization becomes more democratic, as it levels off class distinctions, a happier and more cheerful architecture seems desirable. We are a colorful nation, not a gray one, and the aspect of our buildings ought to reflect this spirit accordingly.

Prudential Life Insurance building, Los Angeles. Pink facing tile has been used for the wings, a color effect that is suitable for the climate and contrasts dramatically with blue skies.

After all, color, like science, represents a conquest of nature. Where civilization reaches its greatest concentration in the large city, where it symbolizes a man-made world, natural building materials seem rather out-of-place. Through the development of ceramics, terra cotta, plastics, and fabricated materials, man creates an art of his own that is better than raw stone for the simple reason that it has taxed his resourcefulness and inventiveness. These substances are his; he has devised them and commanded them. With his electricity and air conditioning, his machines and gadgets, he needs to encompass them in a building that is likewise freed of natural bonds.

View of Library of University of Mexico, Mexico, D. F. A brilliant use of color and design over the entire façade of a building.

Lever House, New York. A tribute to modern materials — as against stone and brick — in which architecture today and in the future has unlimited color possibilities. Skidmore, Owings & Merrill, architects. (Ezra Stoller photograph.)

High school at New Bern, North Carolina. B. H. and R. H. Stephens, architects. Here is a colorful use of ceramic tile that contrasts sharply with the more austere treatment of schools in former years. Courtesy of Cambridge Tile Manufacturing Co. (Cable Studio photograph.)

Home Architecture

Some years ago Frank Lloyd Wright wrote of the ancient use of marble: "The Greeks. . . painted the noble new material entirely out of sight with gorgeous gold and color decorations, themselves, therefore, the original inferior-desecrators." Perhaps the Greeks failed to hold the sentiment of modern times for an inexpensive material to be hewn from the earth. Even more likely, the art of encaustic painting with which they bedecked marble was a complex one, and it demanded a skill which challenged the best minds of the day.

It seems to be a city man's idea that a home in the country ought to look as if it grew out of the earth. Maybe it should. Yet such a fancy may very well be a passing one. The clays used by primitive people, the hides and timbers employed, were for purposes of convenience, not beauty. In the tropics, where

Ceramic tile is one of the most permanent of all colorful materials for the exteriors of buildings.

Fitchberg Library in Massachusetts, with colorful porcelain enamel decorations by Gyorgy Kepes. (Ezra Stoller photograph.)

natural surroundings are vivid, only the bright hue holds interest; therefore, ceramic tile and brilliant textiles are in profusion. A good argument could be centered around a debate as to whether a home in the country should look like an integral part of its natural surroundings or whether it should be in stark contrast. To complement nature, stand apart from it, may also be a worthy expression of man's wish to be independent and superior. To many sensitive minds there is an amusing incongruity between natural stone fireplaces in the living room and freezers and dust precipitators in the kitchen and cellar.

Exterior Color Schemes

Not being an architect, the author hesitates to take sides in any controversies over design. His prejudice, however, is definitely in favor of color and thereby, by simple deduction, against raw stone and rock. The spirit of color

may well be likened to progress in science, for the fabrication of color in building materials requires skillful technology. Why go back into the woods when the trek of progress has been out and away?

If color is to be used, what principles should guide its choice? Today an unoriginal and shallow courage may lead some architects and industrial designers to employ vivid red, yellow, green, blue. Yet such impulsive use of color is hardly to be termed good art or architecture. It is far too naive and blunt.

From remarks already presented it should be recognized that color holds definite relation to form and that it may be manipulated to express structure, weight, spaciousness, distance. Warm colors such as red, orange, yellow are sharply focused and seem appropriate for prominent forms and details seen at a short distance. Cool colors such as green and blue are less sharply focused and lend themselves to large area and simple mass.

Striking colors and simple architectural form are expertly coordinated in the General Motors Technical Center, Warren Township, Michigan. Eero Saarinen, architect.

These cylinders have been arbitrarily shaded. The left one implies bright illumination, and the right one implies dim illumination, even though both may be seen in the same light. Color control like this offers the architect an unusual opportunity to influence the human perception of form.

Dark colors appear heavier than pale colors. Texture is more compelling than plainness. If vivid color is strong and commanding, light grayish tones best suit the upper reaches of high buildings and will appear atmospheric and lofty.

Pure colors will appear luminous in grayish setting. Illumination effects may be conveyed by colors that blend gradually into each other. Subtly different colors on different elevations — preferably warm tones set against cool tones — will artificially produce effects of sunlight and shadow.

Region and Locale

For consistency of mass and form, monochromatic effects with color are perhaps best. Contrast may then be introduced in architectural details about the entrance or lower parts of the building.

In metropolitan areas and in cities having a relatively low percentage of sunlight, grayer tones of color may be preferable to avoid too shocking a contrast on cloudy or misty days. However, the upper areas may be slightly lighter in tint and more luminous in hue to pierce the sky and appear dramatic.

In sunnier regions, stronger color will best feature architecture. Gray looks forlorn in bright sunlight, although white is excellent. Warm hues such as yellow, coral, tan, soft green, and soft blue all hold possibilities.

For good balance, remember that the deep color will appear heavier than the pale color, and that brightness will have greater attraction than darkness. Contrasting hues will tend to cut a building into separate sections and to feature its parts rather than its whole.

Experiment in "passive painting" to reduce the visibility of Navy buildings. Faber Birren, consultant. Special tones of green, gray, and maroon (foreground) lessen the contrast of white (background). The use of colors achieves a desired result without the need for obvious "camouflage."

10

The Effects

of Color

Because architecture and interior design have been dominated by esthetic considerations, and because most books in these fields have stressed the importance of feeling and creative spirit, there may be unique value in a more or less factual story of color and its physiological and psychological effects.

In new days of stress and tension, color will no doubt be asked to serve more important functions than mere beauty. Pleasure may not be enough, even in homes. Less fatigue and nervous tension, greater use of color for the best possible reactions of the human organism, may one day be expected. Healthful degrees of temperature, ideal percentages of humidity, necessary footcandle levels of illumination have all been determined through research and have become acceptable in the building field. Although color reaction is largely emotional, nonetheless it too may be studied objectively. The lessons learned in industry, schools, and hospitals are applicable to other spaces found in hotels and homes. With allowances made for human likes and predilections, color — notably brightness — may be engineered intelligently to make any interior a more comfortable place in which to live, read, work, and relax.

Heliotherapy

Color not only affects the human mood but it causes positive responses throughout the organism. Man not only feels different on a sunny than on a rainy day, but his body reacts differently.

Sun bathing is practiced today as it was centuries ago. In the latter part of the nineteenth century Niels R. Finsen of Denmark studied the effects of natural sunlight and the newly developed carbon arc. He wrote of the actinic properties of light, treated tuberculars, and in 1903 was awarded a Nobel prize. That light could prove therapeutic had its first clinical proof.

In the terms of medicine, radiosensitivity is associated with invisible radiation such as x-rays and radium rays, while photosensitivity is associated with visible light and its adjacent infrared and ultraviolet. On the latter energy — which is most closely related to color — depend health and life.

The human body is particularly responsive to ultraviolet light. Today artificial sources of it are finding wide use in industry, hospitals, and schools. Many plastics transmit this energy of sunlight and are used for fenestration in chicken houses and shelters for domestic animals. Plastic domes and windows would also be desirable in solaria and homes to make sunbathing possible without actual outdoor exposure. Blonds seem to be more sensitive to ultraviolet light than are brunets. In India, rickets is a common affliction among some higher caste Hindus, whose religion requires mothers and children to dwell in complete indoor isolation. The lack of sunlight leads to vitamin D deficiency and hence to disease. Among Eskimo women, menstruation may cease during the long arctic night, and the libido of men may be likewise dormant — a form of human hibernation due to lack of ultraviolet radiation.

Vitamin D is produced by ultraviolet light, which also destroys germs and causes chemical changes in the body. This energy is artificially produced to add vitamins to milk, butter, foodstuffs. It is effectively scattered by atmosphere, and its benefits in sunlight are to be found even in smoky cities, despite popular disbelief. Through exposure to ultraviolet, the skin becomes tanned. Yet too much of it may prove harmful and may be a contributing cause to skin cancer.

As a comment on the atom bomb, this high-frequency radiation is better reflected by light colors than by dark. Thus white or off-white clothing and white exterior walls will prove something of a safeguard when radiation, not concussion, is the destroying factor.

Visible Light

Although therapeutic values of color are seldom admitted, one is not to deny the potency of color entirely. In his work in hospitals the author has never attempted to insist upon a direct therapeutic viewpoint. This is not necessary, for there are enough indirect and psychological values in color to warrant its widespread use for purposes of rapid convalescence, agreeable frame of mind, and healthful living. A few references to them may serve to encourage more study of functional use of color.

At the beginning of this century Oscar Raab of Germany noted the toxicity of dyes. Experimenting with different dye solutions, he discovered that the time required to destroy microscopic organisms was related both to the intensity of light in his laboratory and to the density of his dyestuffs. Organisms exposed to sunlight survived over long periods. However, when dye was introduced, the organisms immediately became light-sensitive and were promptly killed. Although the dye itself was chemically inert, it stained the gelatinous microbes, caused the absorption of ultraviolet rays, and resulted in the death of the microbes.

Plants

One of the curious and inexplicable aspects of color is encountered in the growth of plants. Although rays shorter and longer than visible light are found in the sun's energy, nature has apparently effected a practical balance in which visible light and color are the chief requirements of sound growth and development. Whereas the medical profession recognizes therapy in the invisible energy of infrared and ultraviolet and is skeptical about visible light, among plants visible light is the needed radiation, and infrared and ultraviolet will destroy them.

Color in the growth of plants has been investigated many times over the years. Wholly magical properties were at one time claimed, and greenhouses equipped with colored panes of glass were erected in many parts of Europe and America. In most reports, however, unusual actions were brought about less by the positive effects of hue than by negative ones traceable to reduced light and radiation.

Length of day is highly significant. Flowers and plants belong to long-day and short-day groups. Most grains and vegetables thrive during long summer days. Flowers such as the chrysanthemum require short days. By using electric light to supplement daylight, three generations of wheat have been grown in one year. The extremely long days of summer in Alaska and Canada are responsible for bountiful crops of hay, wheat, and potatoes. Oranges grown in the northern part of California, where the days are longer, reach the market several weeks before those grown a few hundred miles farther south. Certain berries and flowers can be forced to ripen and bloom earlier through control of light, offering commercial advantages and bigger profits to the grower.

As to color itself, most long-day plants seem to have greatest response under red-orange light. With wheat, red rays are most stimulating, then blue, yellow, green. Infrared and ultraviolet contribute nothing and, indeed, will impair growth.

Birds and Animals

Birds are extremely sensitive to color. Many of them even seem to have color preferences. Hummingbirds will feed best from a red container. Poisoned seeds, dyed green, will protect bird life, for to the bird the green seed will appear unripe, while to the color-blind rodent it will resemble any other seed and will be eaten without discrimination.

Bird migration has been partially explained as a phenomenon involving length of day. As the shorter days of autumn approach, a reaction probably takes place in the glandular system of the bird. Migration may even take place before crops and seeds are fully mature.

T. H. Bissonnette has shown that migration and sexual cycles may be influenced by light and color, red light and lengthening days appearing to stimulate activity and actual growth in sexual organs.

Bissonnette has also performed a series of remarkable experiments with animals. The brown weasel, which becomes the white ermine during the short days of winter, has been given a white coat in mid-summer by reducing the creature's exposure to light.

Goats, which (unlike the cow) have a seasonal milk supply, can be made productive at will through control of light. "Results indicate that breeding cycles in goats are controlled by daily periods of light in such a way that short days induce breeding while long days inhibit it."

Human Beings

Human tissue is sensitive to light. Skin eruptions may follow the use of perfumes, ointments, after-shave lotions, such preparations *in some persons* making the flesh light-sensitive and producing a rash. Red dye has been injected into the blood of rachitic children to facilitate better absorption of ultraviolet radiation. It is also believed that many forms of allergy, hives, rash, may be traced to foodstuffs which, through the blood stream, make the skin react unfavorably to light. Sheep have been dyed and painted to withstand intense sunlight. In humans, the chlorophyll of grass crushed on the skin, the handling of parsnips, figs, chemicals, may prove hazardous. In a

The orientation of the human body may be subtly affected by color. Under the influence of red (left), outstretched arms may tend to move outward and be attracted to the stimulus. Under the influence of green or blue (right), there may be withdrawal from the stimulus. After Goldstein.

strange affliction known as urticaria solare, the skin reacts unfavorably to visible blue light.

In experiments conducted abroad several years ago, blue dye solutions painted on wounds accelerated healing because of greater absorption of red and infrared light. These latter forms of radiation have been applied before surgical operations to speed recovery.

Light Tonus

The body has definite reactions to light and color, and a general tonus is to be admitted. The word "tonus" refers to the condition of steady activity maintained by the body. Muscular tension and relaxation, for example, are tonus changes. They are to some extent noticeable and measurable and are a good clue to the action of color, however slight. Red has been found to increase muscular tension and blue to relax it.

When light is shone into one eye, tension may be produced over the corresponding side of the body. It may be concluded that light acts not only on the muscles but is effective in causing changes in the entire organism.

In an experimental method devised by Metzger, Goldstein, and others, a subject is requested to stretch out his arms horizontally in front of his body. When light is shone into one eye, the arms may move toward the illumination. With colored light directed into both eyes, red causes the arms to spread away

from each other. With green and blue, the arms tend to approach each other in a series of jerky motions. "This reaction takes place quite independently of the visual apparatus. It occurs when the eyes are tightly sealed to exclude light and is said to have been observed in blind individuals" (Felix Deutsch).

Some authorities are of the opinion that the body has a radiation sense. The skin may contain cells having close association with the nervous system and a sensitivity to radiant energy. Tonus reflex seems to be in two directions, with yellow-green as a neutral point. Toward red and orange there is attraction to stimulus; toward blue and green there is withdrawal from it. Even infrared and ultraviolet will cause reflex actions.

A few men have been so bold as to venture the opinion that yellow and purple light have the best effect on human metabolism. Red may weaken it considerably and green slightly. The influence of color, weak or strong, depends as well on whether it is seen as brilliant or dim. The pulse is generally slower in darkness than in bright illumination. All too clearly, any color application must hold regard for illumination intensity. If red is a stimulating color, its action may be negated by dim light. And the tranquil qualities of blue may be quite the reverse if it reflects intense light. This may suggest that warm hues, being aggressive and exciting, have most potency in brilliant light, while cool colors, more passive and subduing, lend themselves to suppressed light.

11

The New Psychology

In the emotional realm many abstruse and empirical theories have been propounded. Libraries are replete with books, monographs, and essays on the "spiritual" significance of color. It is to be granted that men throughout history have symbolized color in many strange ways. The experience of color is quite personal and stirring and therefore inspiring of hyperbole and imagination.

In recent years, however, scientists in psychology, physiology, and psychiatry have noted many consistent facts about human reaction to color. The art of color may one day have competent sources for its expression, sources which not only stress talent but which deal resourcefully with known psychological factors in color perception. Designers and decorators may be expected to have a rational grasp of their subject and to qualify their efforts with something more palpable than mere feeling or insight. For color is of tremendous value in dealing with human moods, in promoting greater comfort, and in lessening neurotic tension and anxiety.

General Color Reactions

In most studies of color preference, the order of choice is blue, red, green, purple, yellow, orange. Red will be seen as the most exciting of colors, green as the most tranquil, and blue-violet as the most subduing.

In what is termed the unity of the senses, definite relationships are found between the sensation of color and those of hearing, taste, odor. With music, for example, "The horizontal dimension might be related to the development of music in time; the vertical dimension to changes in pitch. A third dimension of depth may eventually be available to denote volume or intensity" (Theodore F. Karwoski and Henry S. Odbert). This would mean that music moves along quickly or slowly, depending on its tempo. It jumps into tints for high notes or drops down into shades for low notes. When it is fortissimo, the colors are near, intense, heavy. When it is pianissimo, the colors are filmy, grayish, and far away.

In the quality of warmth, red-orange is seen as the "hottest" of colors, while the range for "coolness" is broader and extends from blue-green to blue to violet. In the sense of taste, the "appetizing" hues are warm red, pale yellow, peach, clear green, tan, and certain browns. Yellow-green, purple, and gray seem unsavory. Pink is "sweet."

Color Preference

The relationships existing between color preference and personality are many indeed and they are quite fascinating to study. As many psychiatrists and psychologists have noted in the sense of vision, response to form seems to arouse intellectual processes, while reactions to color are more impulsive and emotional. Small children, for example, are "color dominant" more than "form dominant." In classical experiments devised by Gestalt psychologists, the ambiguous task of matching a green disk against an assortment of red disks and green triangles will readily be attempted on a basis of color by children. Adults will be hesitant and will point to the discrepancy. David Katz writes, "Color, rather than shape, is more closely related to emotion."

This primitive quality of color has been referred to by numerous investigators. Maria Rickers-Ovsiankina writes in connection with the Rorschach method used to probe the depths of human personality, "Color experience, when it occurs, is thus a much more immediate and direct sense datum than the experience of form. For perception is usually accompanied by a detached, objective attitude in the subject. Whereas the experience of color, being more immediate, is likely to contain personal, affectively toned notes."

In interpreting the art expression of young children from three to five years of age, Alschuler and Hattwick concluded that a delight in color showed emotional tendencies, and the frequent use of blue or black indicated self-control and the repression of emotion. As might be expected, red had the highest affective value and revealed uninhibited expression. Yellow seemed to go with infantile traits and dependence on grownups. Green showed balance, fewer emotional impulses, a simple and uncomplicated nature.

In a broad way the spectrum may be divided into colors of long wave length (red, orange) and colors of short wave length (green, blue), with yellow occupying a middle position. A number of researchers have called attention to the fact that human beings tend to fall into two distinct groups — those preferring clear, distinct hues, usually warm in tone, and those who favor cooler hues and tones of less saturation. "The warm color dominant subjects are characterized by an intimate relation to the visually perceptible world. They are receptive and open to outside influences. They seem to submerge themselves rather readily in their social environment. Their emotional life is characterized by warm feelings, suggestibility, and strong affects. All mental functions are rapid and highly integrated with each other. In the subject-object relationship, the emphasis is on the object. The cold color dominant subjects . . . have a detached 'split-off' attitude to the outside world. They find it difficult to adapt themselves to new circumstances and to express themselves freely. Emotionally they are cold and reserved. In the subject-object relationship, the emphasis is on the subject" (Maria Rickers-Ovsiankina).

Emotionally the red end of the spectrum is exciting; the blue end is subduing. Physically and physiologically, the same sort of complementation exists. Red colors tend to increase bodily tension, to stimulate the autonomic nervous system, but green and blue colors release tension and have a lesser physiological effect. It is to be granted, of course, that direct connections exist between the brain and the body and that reactions take place independently of thought or deliberation.

The rather striking observation is to be made that the division of the spectrum into warm and cool colors holds very evident and simple meaning with reference to human personality. Colors seem to differ as psychic makeup differs. According to the general observations of Jaensch, with the warm color goes the primitive response of children, excitation, the extroverted human being, the predilection of the brunet complexion type. With the cool color goes the more mature response, tranquilization, the introverted being, the predilection of the blond complexion type. Indeed, though the conclusion may be largely empirical, warmth and coolness in color are dynamic qualities, warmth signifying contact with environment, coolness signifying withdrawal into oneself.

Emotional Significance

By and large, emotional reactions are not easy to measure. However, color is of much psychiatric importance and its mysteries are quite deserving of study. "The fact that a certain relation exists between character and color preference has become evident from so many experiments that further proof is hardly required" (Kouwer). Yet it is well known that emotional attitudes often are difficult to reduce to formal analysis. The criteria of scientific proof may be quite at variance with ordinary experience. This is particularly true of color, for where emphasis may be shifted from simple, emotional enjoyment to rational contemplation, "facts" may be distorted, invalidated, or entirely lost.

It is unquestionably a normal condition for human beings to like color. There are precise reactions and "moods" to be associated with sunny weather and with rainy weather, with a colorful world or environment and with a drab one. Yet in adults, excessive verbosity or "longing" for color may be an indication of mental confusion, for as a person grows older, interest in form quite naturally exceeds interest in color. Where there may be insistence upon balanced relationships between color and form, one probably has encountered a person who is willing to admit an emotional life but who is determined to keep it within the bonds of reason.

A person who, in general, reacts freely and agreeably to colors — any and all — is likely to have a responsive personality and to be keenly interested in if not well oriented toward the world at large. His less enthusiastic neighbor may be of solemn countenance and glum disposition. Persons having an agreeable rapport with the outer world will like color; those given to inner rapport may not.

Personality Types

If, then, love of color is a sign of outwardly directed interests, and if indifference to color is significant of introspective tendencies, a basic though

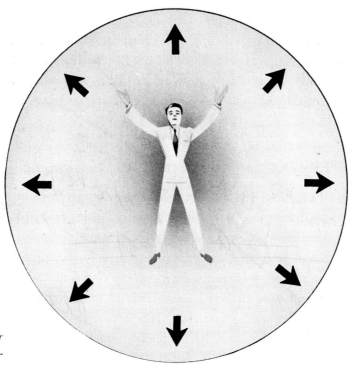

Bright colors in an interior may create an outward attraction and stimulate muscular activity. Soft colors permit attention to be directed inward and aid visual and mental concentration.

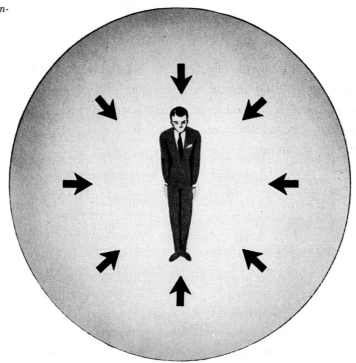

simple lesson is learned. In studies of the effects of alcohol, the release of inhibitions in the severely introverted mortal is accompanied by a greater response to color. Again, it may be noted in empirical observation that abstract, non-objective, and surrealistic art forms tend to have a greater acceptance among extroverts than among introverts. The outwardly oriented individual may appreciate color for the sake of color; those who are inwardly oriented require a semblance of realism if art forms are to appeal and make "sense."

It may thus be generally assumed that emotionally responsive persons will react freely to color; inhibited mortals may be shocked or embarrassed by it; restricted and detached types may be unaffected.

Among the mentally ill, the significance of color has been extensively noted in case studies developed out of the Rorschach technique. There may be a reversion to childish fancies toward color. In the "ink-blots" of the Rorschach test cards, sight of the hued designs may cause great exuberance. Manic-

"Ink blots" of the type shown here are used by psychiatrists in the Rorschach test to study personality traits and disturbances. Extroverts are likely to think concretely, and introverts tend to think abstractly.

113

depressives in particular will be pleased by color and will react with considerable (and agreeable) excitement to it.

In many forms of mental disturbance, on the other hand, color may be looked upon as an intruding and disturbing element. The person may be visibly upset. He may reject the color as he would pain, close his eyes, turn from it, or perhaps try to destroy it. Color shock of this nature, however, is seldom noted in manic-depressives.

Schizophrenic types are inclined to reject color, to look upon it as something which may prove "catastrophic" and break in upon their inner world. Looking at the test cards, they may volunteer a few vague remarks about form but be silent as to color.

In severe depressive states of psychotic degree, the rejection of color may be of a negative order, the person preferring a "gray" world and disdaining a colorful one. Those having the severest psychiatric defects will, as a rule, react to color but will seldom if ever see anything coherent in it.

Among epileptics, Rorschach himself noted that color response increased with the progress of disease and that it might conceivably be looked upon as a scale expressing degree of deterioration.

The Mentally Ill

One of the real problems in psychiatry is to mark distinctions between psychotic reactions in which contact with reality may be lost and neurotic reactions in which contact with reality is maintained. Differences are perhaps more in degree of severity, although some clinical differences may exist.

Among emotionally disturbed persons (neurotics), it is not so much the favorable color response as the unfavorable one which sets them quite apart from normal persons. In writing of the Rorschach test cards, Klopfer and Kelley state, "Probably the most important single sign of a neurotic reaction is color shock; . . . neurotics invariably show such shock, and only a small percentage of normals and other types of psychopathology display it."

Hysterical persons may find it difficult to organize their thoughts coherently when color is an element to be considered. The same appears true of the organically confused subject suffering from neurasthenia and exhaustion. The presence of color on the Rorschach card may elicit no more than a matter-of-fact naming of the hues, with no attempt to expose the content of thought. In anxiety states and obsessive neuroses, profound color shock may also be shown. The willingness of the hysteric to be affected by color is, perhaps, indicative of his egocentricity.

How is color shock to be explained? In an unusual study of color-blind neurotics, Brosin and Fromm concluded that a "brain effect" was encountered. In other words, the neurotic may react to color without having a clear perception of it. "This physical stimulus need not necessarily be in the field of awareness." This conclusion would seem to be true, for the reaction of the human organism to color is a complex affair whose *gestalt* embraces the entire physical body. Sensitivity to color has been noted even in totally blind individuals.

The Meaning of Individual Colors

To quote from an article by Eric P. Mosse, "The difference between mental health and mental disease consists at last in nothing else but how this predicament is handled. The normally balanced individuum will face, brace and adapt himself to his problems, whereas mental disease is the manifestation of different depths of escape. With this fact in mind, we automatically understand why in achromatopsia of the hysterical the order in which the colors disappear is violet, green, blue and finally red. Aside and above this experience we generally found in hysterical patients, especially in psychoneuroses with anxiety states, a predilection for green as symbolizing the mentioned escape mechanism. The emotional attack of the outside is repressed, the 'red' impulses of hatred, aggression and sex denied. . . . For the same reason we will not be surprised that *red* is the color of choice of the manic and hypomanic patient giving the tumult of his emotions their 'burning' and 'bloody' expression. And we don't wonder that melancholia and depression reveal themselves through a complete 'black out.' Finally we see yellow as the color of schizophrenia. . . . This yellow is the proper and intrinsic color of the morbid mind. Whenever we observe its accumulative appearance we may be sure that we are dealing with a deep lying psychotic disturbance." Mosse further related brown to paranoia.

Without being too symbolic, we may say that a preference for red is associated with an outwardly integrated personality or with a person who nourishes a desire to be well adjusted to the world. Red indicates extroversion and is highly prized by persons of vital temperament. Such persons may not be too reflective and may be more ruled by impulse than by deliberation. In mental disease and psychoneuroses, red is to be associated with manic tendencies, as Mosse and others have remarked.

The writer's experience would ally yellow with extreme mental disturbance (genius or feeble-mindedness) rather than with schizophrenia. (Schizophrenics generally prefer blue.) It is likely to be preferred by persons having an intellectual bent. In other words, yellow may be looked upon as an intellectual color, associated both with great intelligence and mental deficiency. Vincent Van Gogh's attraction to the hue is notable in many of his paintings, particularly in those executed in the latter years of his life.

Green, with a generous empirical viewpoint, may be associated with Freud's oral character. At least, it is often the choice of the persons who are superficially intelligent and social, who are given to voluble habits of speech, and who often have an intense appetite for food. To the psychoneurotic and psychotic, green is a great favorite. Probably it suggests escape from anxiety, sanctuary in the untroubled greenness of nature. Under stress those who prefer green will not as a rule crave seclusion; on the contrary they may seek out and need companionship.

It is the writer's personal conviction that narcissism is, in a surprisingly high percentage of cases, revealed by a preference for blue-green. Where an average mortal will like either green or blue, the choice of blue-green may indicate fastidiousness, sensitiveness, and discrimination.

Blue is the color associated with schizophrenia. A majority of inwardly-integrated personalities will favor the color, for it is allied with a profound control of emotions. Here is the color of circumspection. Under stress persons who like blue may tend to make a tragic flight from environment.

With brown the anal character of Freud is fairly well symbolized: conscientiousness, parsimony, obstinacy. Brown, of course, is to be associated with human excrement.

There are many other aspects to color preferences. Convivial persons may be attached to orange; artistic persons may prefer purple. A well disciplined red personality may confess his imposed training by a preference for maroon. In what the psychiatrist terms the liberation of repressed effects, a meek, shy soul may take to brilliant hues with "fire in his eyes." The aggressive mortal to whom life has been a tough and harsh struggle may be drawn to the tint of pink. To him pink may be a bright symbol of an unconscious wish for gentility.

Color and Psychotherapy

To be more practical again, what scientific value (if any) does color have in architecture and decoration? What principles are to be deduced from a study of preferences, of psychoneuroses and mental disturbances?

For the most part, color therapy has been skeptically regarded in America.

Despite a rather unfair prejudice, however, only an iconoclast would entirely deny potency in the hues of the spectrum.

Based on a good fund of technical research and scientific study, the therapeutic application of color to homes, hospitals, schools, and the like has a fairly reliable basis. Here are a few salient features.

In general, bright light and warm colors represent an attraction to stimulus, a tendency for the human organism to direct its activities outwardly and to take action. Softer illumination and cool colors represent a withdrawal from the outer world. They tend to drive the individual within himself and to inspire introspection. If brightness and warmth stimulate action, then dimness and coolness will provide an ideal setting for the execution of tasks.

The significance of all this has been well expressed by Kurt Goldstein: "One could say *red is inciting to activity and favorable for emotionally determined actions; green creates the condition of meditation and exact fulfillment of the task. Red may be suited to produce the background out of which ideas and actions will emerge; in green these ideas will be developed and the actions executed.*"

Interior Design

Among *normal* humans it is a fallacious tradition (shared by most interior designers and decorators) to recommend cool colors for excitable persons and warm colors for phlegmatic ones. In small children, a pacific environment and pacific attitude may serve only to increase tension and prod irritability. Bright color may relieve nervousness by creating an outward stimulus to balance an inner and wholly natural fervor. Conversely, in melancholy humans an attempt to "cheer up" a mood of dejection (through color or anything else) may serve merely to aggravate the misery and drive it even deeper. For most of us an extroverted temperament may be content in a bright and colorful environment, but an introverted temperament may find greatest peace in a more sedate and conservative setting.

Yet where neurotic and psychotic patients are concerned, the prescriptions may have to be reversed. Here the author speaks largely from his own experience and from the results of many contacts with psychiatrists. Patients in a frantic and manic state may require sedation with color — blue and green tones — and dim illumination. The extremely melancholic may need a compensating warmth of hue and brightness of light.

12

Stores, Hotels, and Restaurants

Where the color problem involves public appeal and where functionalism as such is not a major requisite, the approach may well contemplate a study of average preferences. To project personal likes and dislikes is, once more, to assume certain risks. The individual taste of an architect or decorator may or may not appeal to others. Thus too much of the "creative spirit," too much originality, may lead to effects which appear strange if not objectionable.

Human taste is simple and may be given two distinct classifications. In high fashion markets catering to a sophisticated clientele — dress shops and specialty stores, cocktail lounges, expensive hotels and restaurants situated in large metropolitan areas — color may be treated with high individuality. Here there may be enough "customers" to draw upon who will relish a sense of exclusiveness and offer their patronage because they favor that which is not meant for the public at large.

In women's fashions, for example, there is a top but limited market for unusual styles. These women will buy merchandise (a) if it is different, (b) if they do not now have it, and (c) if they are assured that no one else has it. These same persons, men included, will seek out shops and clubs

View of Burdine's, Miami Beach, designed by Raymond Loewy Associates. One of America's top design organizations has ably handled the complex problem of store decoration, exploiting color for maximum appeal and merchandising power. (Gottscho-Schleisner photograph.)

having restricted patronage. It is here that architects and decorators may give free reign to their impulses, for here the exceptional is respected.

Mass Taste

Highly individual designers very often fail when they attempt to style mass market consumer goods. Average Americans are quite the opposite of sophisticated ones. They like what everyone else likes and want what everyone else has. Although the styles that attract them unquestionably come from upper class markets, this distinction alone is not enough, for out of a dozen or more colors and styles advanced by the "favored few," only a few ever survive. The rest fall by the wayside — and no amount of promotion will make them successful.

The reason, perhaps, is that people with high income and exclusive taste are mental and deliberate in their choices; the masses of people are more emotional and are motivated less by thought than by inner compulsions. The masses are influenced by general trends and are prone to want the same things and to be attracted to the same styles and colors in merchandise as well as architecture.

Neiman Marcus, Dallas. Eleanor LeMaire, designer. An effective use of natural materials: green marble walls, brownish terrazzo floor, redwood stanchions, and natural wood escalator panels. (Ezra Stoller photograph.)

Neiman Marcus store, Dallas. Eleanor LeMaire, designer. Here is a rich and resourceful use of color: pale lime ceiling, brown and gold terrazzo floor, walls in soft yellow, wood paneling in bronze green and redwood. (Ezra Stoller photograph.)

Two Case Histories

Illustrating the difference between high fashion and mass taste, two simple case histories may be cited. In the first, a once successful but rather dowdy restaurant was completely rehabilitated. The exterior was redone in brightly hued mosaic having a modern and unrealistically abstract design. The interior was refurnished with extreme taste, exotic colors, extravagantly chosen furnishings and draperies. This restaurant, which catered to average persons and was in the nature of a coffee shop, promptly saw its trade

dwindle. Within a few months — and no doubt at great expense — it was remodeled a second time, the exterior façade treated with red brick and colonial trim, the interior with more traditional furnishings.

It is not difficult to appreciate what happened. The first rehabilitation constituted an effect that jarred the nerves and simple taste of the public. The modern style ran contrary to what is popularly liked and understood. It is not that the work of the architect and designer was bad but that it was wrong and improperly conceived for the class of persons to which it was meant to appeal.

Unusual color and unusual design in themselves hold little meaning unless by chance — or by analysis — they have universal elements of beauty.

To cite a second example, the Capital Transit Company of Washington, D. C. recently called upon a group of designers to style a series of street cars. Management itself held the conviction that the public wanted its hues bold and startling. Yet in a final poll of the public itself, an extremely conservative effect designed by the author won majority approval. The interior was blue-green, with a maroon feature stripe, tan upholstery and tan flooring. Other cars in multicolor combinations with two-tone seats and inlaid floors hardly entered the reckoning.

It is a mistaken opinion, held by some artists, that the public has gaudy taste. The average American home, for example, reflects conservative Colonialism, not European modernism. To say that such taste is bad is to speak out-of-turn. What is wrong, if anything, is that mass styling is too often left to poor designers. The man of better taste too frequently refuses to think objectively, to seek common denominators, and to improve upon them.

After all, sophisticated taste is what is ephemeral. Mass taste, reflected in peasant styles and native art forms, is what endures through the years and is constantly revived to great success.

Store Decoration

The American public has simple taste. It likes its colors plain, clear, direct in their appeal. It is almost elemental to say that the appearance of the store itself should not run contrary in color to the tints of the products it sells. And the same careful research that guides the styling of consumer goods should also guide the choice of color for the store interior.

The most obvious mistake is to overstyle an interior. Decorate it with purples, yellow-greens, browns, and deep grays, and the public may take

Restaurant at Bloomingdale's, Stamford, Connecticut. Raymond Loewy Associates, designers. A fresh, cheerful effect is achieved with bleached wood and pink walls and furniture in pastel tints.

Pierre Grille, Hotel Pierre, New York. Unusual decorations by Edgar Miller are engraved in gold leaf. Lighting is soft and mellow. (Lionel Freedman photograph.)

one look, turn on its heel, and go somewhere else. Why not? How can the store, in its decoration, contradict the styling of the products it sells? Note how strangers in a city cup their hands over their eyes to peer into the interiors of shops and restaurants. First impressions are vital; quick general reactions will attract or repel trade, depending on how they strike human emotions.

What safe principles may be followed? First of all, illumination. Brightness attracts the eye, compels attention, and invites traffic.

In a store, good brightness engineering should be utilized. Upper walls, for example, should not be too light. Reflectances around 50 per cent are recommended. If upper walls are exceedingly pale, attention may go up and away from the merchandise displayed. Indeed, the pupil of the eye may be unduly constricted, and the perception of dark colored merchandise may be handicapped.

Ceilings may be white for high light reflection. Floors and fixtures should also be fairly bright, with a reflectance of about 20 or 25 per cent.

As to color choice, very few colors hold universal interest: red, yellow, green, blue, ivory, peach, pink, maroon, navy, tan, gray, and possibly turquoise, chartreuse, and beige. Beyond these, other colors may appear unemotionally subtle.

For general merchandising areas, soft tones of green and peach are usually attractive, even though commonplace. Fixtures may be in gray or blue.

For special departments, a medium tone of grayish blue-green is one of the best for women's fashions. Its hue complements the pinkish tint of human complexion, and its medium tone gives an almost equal visibility to light and dark garments. For dramatic emphasis in displays, fixtures, and end walls, the most satisfying deep colors are forest green, blue, and maroon.

Blue is useful in appealing to men, rose and pink in appealing to women. Conventional though these colors may be, research studies have shown them to be both practical and profitable. If blue, rose, and pink outsell most other hues in consumer goods — esthetic taste to the contrary — then they are equally useful in store decoration. The good architect and designer will take pains to express good taste, seek uncommon variations of popular colors, and harmonize them in resourceful ways.

For foods, white is the ideal finish for counters and refrigerated cabinets. Blue and blue-green may be used on walls adjacent to meats, peach on walls adjacent to vegetables. Shelf goods may have cases trimmed with the ever-preferred (and non-distracting) blue, with the interiors and backs of shelves white to assure high visibility for packaged goods.

In long narrow stores, yellow may be placed at the rear wall to "pull" the eye directly and the feet indirectly. Around elevators it encourages wider store traffic. Yellow may also be effectively used in basement areas.

Directional light may be necessary to give a desired sparkle to merchandise such as ceramics, glassware, silverware and jewelry; blue is frequently the best background for this merchandise. Chartreuse is good for a flower shop; peach with blue for bakeries; white for automobile showrooms; maroon, forest green, and navy for small alcoves devoted to clothing and furs; rose for home furnishings.

Soft colors (except for yellow) are preferred because they look well over large areas and they set up an excellent background for merchandise.

One good practice is to use a light pearl gray as a general wall color and to contrast it with brighter and deeper hues over end walls, alcoves, and areas back of certain departments and displays. This device will serve the purpose of directing attention to important spaces, and the gray will permit bright and interesting sequences with minimum danger of color clash.

Sectional Preferences

Color preferences are to some extent influenced by duration and degree of sunlight. Where there is prevalent and intense sunlight, people like bright colors in general and warm colors in particular. Conversely, people in more cloudy regions are likely to favor softer and grayer colors and cool ones. Thus warm colors — red, peach, rose, yellow, tan — make ideal building exteriors in sunny climates, with store interiors in cool tones of green and turquoise. Blue, soft green, and gray make ideal exteriors for cloudy regions, with store interiors in warm tones of yellow, peach, pink, rose, and tan.

Hotel Decoration

The use of color in hotels involves far more complications because of different architectural styles and because of different classes of trade. Yet once again choice of color should pay regard to average preferences. The ordinary mortal may feel ill at ease if the color scheme is too extreme, however inspired it is.

As to illumination, soft general light seems best for the lobby, with concentrated light in certain important areas. Warm colors rather than cool ones

COLOR STANDARDS

In most functional color applications many standards are not necessary. Those shown on this color card have all been extensively and successfully specified by Faber Birren. In homes, where greater freedom may be wanted, color choice itself is usually less difficult than deciding upon precise tone. The suggestions herewith may be safely used with good assurance of harmony. (Chart through courtesy of Finishes Division, E. I. du Pont de Nemours & Co., Inc., Wilmington, Del.)

FUNCTIONAL COLORS

FOR FACTORIES, OFFICES, SCHOOLS, HOSPITALS

IVORY

DAYLIGHT GREEN

LIGHT BLUE

SUNLIGHT

DUSK GREEN

GUARDS GRAY

PEACH

LIGHT BLUE-GREEN

LIGHT GRAY

TERRA COTTA

MEDIUM BLUE-GREEN

MEDIUM GRAY

MACHINERY COLORS

HORIZON GRAY

MACHINE TOOL GRAY

DEEP GREEN

SAFETY AND IDENTIFICATION COLORS

HIGH VISIBILITY YELLOW

ALERT ORANGE

FIRE PROTECTION RED

SAFETY GREEN

PRECAUTION BLUE

DECORATIVE COLORS

FOR STORES, HOTELS, RESTAURANTS, HOMES

CANDY PINK	MIST BLUE	LIME
FLAMINGO	SMOKY BLUE	FLESH
LIGHT SAGE	BEIGE	LILAC
MEDIUM SAGE	SANDALWOOD	SPRING GREEN
BUTTER YELLOW	COPPER	FOREST GREEN
SULPHUR YELLOW	SUMMER BLUE	CARDINAL
AQUA	LIGHT ROSE	MIDDY BLUE
TURQUOISE	MEDIUM ROSE	GOLD

are appropriate for a friendly atmosphere. Wall colors should be medium in tone and not too dark. Bright illumination may be prescribed for the coffee shop, with light colors on walls. The cocktail lounge and dining room should have dimmer illumination and softer hues, with incandescent lamps on individual tables and warmly tinted walls to reflect a flattering glow.

In rooms and suites, colors with a reflectance of about 50 per cent are ideal. If they have a slightly grayish cast, they will be more comfortable and less likely to soil. The practice of using wallpaper or deep colors over end walls and alcoves is excellent for interest and variety. Gray makes a good foil color, with end walls in yellow, pink, or chartreuse for normally dark rooms, and medium or deep green, blue or maroon for rooms having fairly strong natural daylight. In hotels, the warm tones may be used on north and east exposures, the cool tones on south and west exposures.

Sunlight distribution in the United States. Color preferences seem to be influenced by weather. Strong warm colors will be favored in sunny regions. Soft cool colors will be favored in relatively cloudy regions.

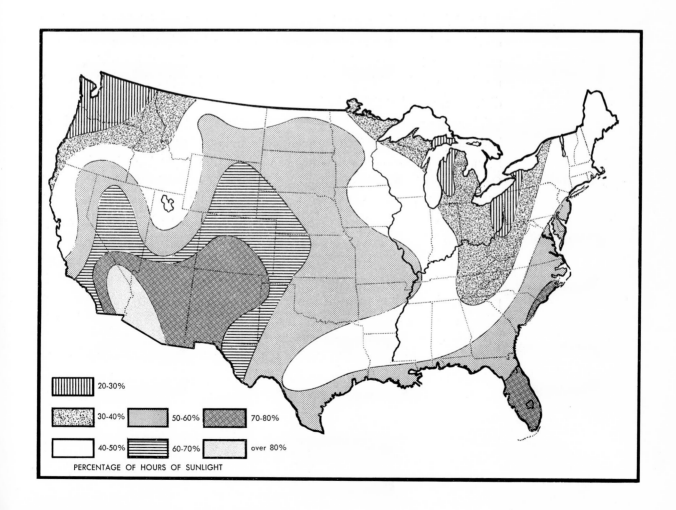

20-30%

30-40% 50-60% 70-80%

40-50% 60-70% over 80%

PERCENTAGE OF HOURS OF SUNLIGHT

For rooms painted one color throughout, the most liked colors are gray, green, rose, and beige. Blue may appear too bleak and melancholy. Peach and pink are best for bathrooms and dressing rooms, to take full advantage of warm reflections.

Furnishings are best when held in contrast — warm rugs and fabrics for cool walls, cool rugs and fabrics for warm walls. Orthodox principles of color harmony are not advised because most persons have a simple and restricted color preference which may collide with academic hue arrangements.

Corridors are proposed in bright, luminous tones of pink, peach, yellow, or tan. In service areas, white walls are desirable for food service, green for the laundry, yellow or white for mechanical shops.

Restaurant Decoration

Good meals make a good restaurant. Yet humans are mighty fussy about service, and even the most delectable fare may be rejected in a smelly and unkempt environment. If the odor of broiled steak whets the appetite, that of rancid fat repels it. If a scrubbed table or bleached cloth enhances the spread, dirt, grease, and stains ruin it.

There are good and bad colors for restaurants, just as there is good and bad housekeeping. Associations between foods and colors are critical. Butter must be neither goldenrod in hue nor too white like vegetable oil substitutes. Oranges are frequently dyed to give them an apparently sweet richness. A Western baker who once produced tinted bread in blue, green, and pink found the venture a dismal failure. A person does not wish to swallow anything that looks unsavory.

Yellowish "pea" greens, for example, have a bilious aspect, even though thousands of cheaper American restaurants are bedecked with it. High style purples, charcoal grays, olive greens, bluish browns — favored by some elite decorators — similarly distress the palate and have led to a drop in patronage.

It may be said that cool colors and bright lights seem appropriate to the coffee shop and lunch counter, whereas warm colors and dim lights are for the more luxurious dining room. In the former instance, the generally bright and cool setting appears clean, and a person eats quickly and gets out. In the latter instance, the warm, subdued setting places the customer at ease, invites a prolonged stay, and presumably helps to increase the size of his check.

Where illumination is bright, then pale green, blue, or ivory are suitable, with fixtures and upholstery in warm red or tan. It is always wise to consider whether or not the colors seem appetizing. Where the illumination is dim, soft tones of rose, grayish green, deep blue, maroon — even vermilion red — will offer possibilities. With white trim and decorations, white tablecloths, and with table lamps or candles, the meal served will be dramatically featured, and conversation and attention will not be distracted by the competition of glaring walls.

For the most part, fluorescent light sources should be avoided except, possibly, for coves. The conventional incandescent lamp has the glint of firelight and is hardly to be surpassed as a light source.

In commercial fields, color finds measurable justification. Although it may be difficult to find criteria for fine art forms — traditional or modern, realistic or abstract — confusion and controversy may be set aside in business. Here beautiful colors are those which sell the most merchandise or attract the most customers. In brief, the right colors are those which are profitable, and the wrong colors are those which are not.

13

Modern Home

Interiors

In a previous chapter, reference was made to the curious relationships existing between color preference and human personality. Here is a new field of inquiry and a new approach opened to designers and decorators which the author terms psychodécor.

Where esthetics are concerned, as in the home, the limits of color expression are boundless. The ancient would rely on symbolism and mythology for his color themes. The sensuousness of the Renaissance gave freer reign to the spectrum and established a veritable free-for-all. Then came tradition and formalized period styles, to be encountered finally by a "modernism" which chose to renounce old amenities and to start anew with a fresh attitude.

Yet if there is such a thing as a modern style in color, there is not much to say in favor of it. Some designers mistake audacity for originality. What with black walls, red ceilings, shockingly brilliant hues, one may say that such impulsiveness matches the fervid spirit of the times, but it hardly marks a profound or meaningful art.

For that matter, a great many modern interiors, with their sharp brightness contrasts, are visually and emotionally distressing. They miss their purpose and they fail to take advantage of much that psychologists and psychiatrists have learned.

Any comments on color in the interior design of homes — by the author or by anyone else — may be readily criticized. Books on the subject are ever at loggerheads. The designer will always do as he pleases. Yet in the interest of a new enlightenment, let some of the major principles of psychodécor be set forth — to be accepted or rejected as the temper chooses.

Steinbrueck house, Seattle. Victor Steinbrueck, archi-
tect. Here is Northwest architecture at its best —
secure, sheltered, and yet light and airy in feeling, with
an abundant variety of visual interests in color and
materials. (Dearborn-Massar photograph.)

Robie house, Chicago, circa 1909, designed in all details by Frank Lloyd Wright. Note table, chairs, lighting fixtures. Colors reflected a frank respect for natural materials and hues. Courtesy of Museum of Modern Art, New York.

Taliesin West (1911-25), home of Frank Lloyd Wright. Again, a simple glorification of natural tones. Courtesy of Museum of Modern Art, New York.

Color Conditioning

Any use of color in the home ought to assure comfort and relaxation. As learned by experience in industry and by research in physiological optics, great differences in brightness (particularly under strong light) are visually trying. They constrict the pupil, cause needless fatigue, and lead to nervousness and irritability. Thus good looking or not, contrasting large areas of black on white — or the equivalent — are as objectionable as exposed electric light bulbs or harsh blasts from radios and television sets.

The curious phenomenon of color constancy involves the remarkable ability of the eye to see a color such as white as normal under widely varying conditions of light intensity. White will be white out in the sun as well as in the dim recesses of a closet. Yet colors and brightnesses change as illumination grows dim, and here most architects and designers are quite uninformed. Many living rooms are designed for evening conditions, the colors being seen under a few footcandles of feeble light. Yet these same spaces may have their colors chosen as though seen under full daylight.

Although all colors and all degrees of brightness are readily seen in bright light, strange things happen when the light is dimmed. Primarily, all medium and deep colors tend to melt together and resemble each other. All colors reflecting less than 20 per cent (and this means about half of all colors capable of being distinguished) will tend to have a uniform brightness. If the illumination conditions of a room are to be on the dim side, there is little reason to expect dark wall colors to have much significance. They won't unless showered with light. Therefore many living rooms have a drab and hollow appearance, despite their promised beauty in sketch or paint and fabric sample.

Emotional Reactions

Although the author insists that color schemes for homes should be geared to the personality of their occupants, there are certain words of advice to be offered. Yellow-green in an aeroplane has been known to aggravate nausea. Large areas of intense ultramarine blue may make the eye so nearsighted that the head feels dizzy. Brilliant red under strong illumination may cause a distressing restlessness, and its green afterimage may give all things in sight a sickening aspect. Reflections from lemon yellow walls may produce a psychological form of jaundice that may make a person sick to his stomach. An overabundance of white may so constrict the pupil of the eye that sharp pains across the forehead are felt.

Dupree house, Akron, Ohio. Robert Little, architect. A rare feeling for beauty of texture exists in this modern home. There is resourceful use of stone, ceramics, wood, paint, and varied fabrics and materials. (Lionel Freedman photograph.)

These may all involve wholly real and literal experiences, fully explicable when the disturbing factors are understood. Persons have been known to feel uncomfortable in a room having a dark or black ceiling. The monotonous regularity of certain conventional wallpaper designs has "gotten on the nerves" of sensitive people. In several reported cases, bright areas of vivid color have impaired production and led to minor accidents because of meaningless distraction.

Color should be emotionally suited to human personality. The point has previously been made that conservative persons (inwardly integrated) have a natural predilection for tradition and sentiment in decoration and for soft, subdued hues, preferably cool. More dynamic souls (outwardly integrated) can appreciate modern, abstract, and more radical design, and with it a bolder array of sharp hues and color contrasts. Many decorators are inclined to miss the fact that the impulsiveness of the extrovert should not be forced upon the introvert. To say that a shy and timid mortal should use bright red is poor advice, for the embarrassment accompanying any such rash display will serve only to increase shyness. Quiet beings are best relaxed in a quiet setting, and here indeed they will find the greatest courage and release.

As to the extrovert, conservatism will not as a rule hold much appeal anyhow, and being given to frank opinions, he will not accept it.

Neurotic Persons

One psychiatrist has called attention to possible color therapy among alcoholics. Medically speaking, such persons are nearly always severely depressed and excessively timorous. Their homes are usually drab and colorless because they resent the intrusion of color and are inclined to take a melancholy and bitter attitude. If they can be prevailed upon to brighten up their environment with strong color, it may well be that desires for alcohol could be lessened. Liquor turns them into extroverts, and color may stand a good chance of diverting their interests from their inner misery to the external surroundings in which they dwell.

The repainting of hospital rooms and wards has had notable results, which have been far more than temporary. In one study, empirical observations revealed that visitors too were impressed. And because of the sensitive reaction of sick patients to the apprehensions of their immediate relatives, convalescence may conceivably be aided.

There is a vital relationship between sickness and frame of mind. Although ultraviolet lamps may have the same action as sunlight, treatment with artificial sources in some dim room will by no means be as therapeutic as that treatment taken on the porch of a sanatorium overlooking green fields, blue skies, and purple mountains. Attractive surroundings, especially those which have been adjusted with care to the "heart's desire" of an individual, unquestionably are salubrious. They will help cure the sick and they will assure good health and cheer to the normal.

Psychodécor in Homes

A color expert is perhaps the last person who should tell a woman how to decorate her home. Nonetheless, a scientific viewpoint is possible and may hold interest to the readers of this book, if only to remind architects and de-

corators that reason and purpose may support a quest for beauty. There are functions to be served in the choice of color.

In living rooms, for example, one may seek comfort, relaxation, and a convivial mood. For conservative mortals, soft tones of rose or warm green may be ideal. There should be a minimum of contrast. As to illumination, some general light should exist to soften shadows. Most light, however, should come from lamps equipped with warm tinted shades. If wall brightness measures between 25 and 40 per cent reflectance, attention will be drawn to the furnishings of the room and to the guests. The rose or warm green tones may be carried out in walls, carpets, and draperies. Other furnishings and upholstery may then be handled in gentle contrast — soft blues and greens for the rose interior, soft golds, rose, and tan for the green interior.

For a livelier effect, the carpets and draperies may be in contrast with the walls, again following the above harmonies.

For a more modern and dramatic result, walls may be gray, with light red, chartreuse, emerald green, blue, turquoise, white applied to end walls, carpets, furnishings. White itself — regardless of vogue — is seldom appropriate in large areas for rooms occupied over long periods of time. It tends to create glare and, by contrast, to give a muddy appearance to colored materials and to human complexion. (White may be suitable, however, for bedrooms and sun rooms.) It will also draw attention to the room in general and may thereby distract from important and proud details.

In normal illumination the human eye will have a clear sense of color values. In dim illumination, however, medium and deep tones will tend to blend together. Lighting conditions will thus have great influence on color "balance."

Other Rooms

In the dining room, attention may be paid to the appetizing qualities of foods. Blue is a good color by way of contrast. Walls and furnishings can be made to look "good enough to eat" by using peach, coral, light clear green, pale yellow, vermilion, tan, brown. Again, conservative persons may prefer monotone effects, while extroverts may prefer contrast. Localized light over the table itself will enhance the meal. There should be a soft glow throughout the room to destroy harsh shadows. The color quality of artificial light should be pinkish or coral, like the flickering warmth of a fireplace.

In bedrooms, brighter colors — warm or cool — may be satisfactory. The cool, soft effect may be best for the introvert, the sharp, crisp hue for the extrovert. Agreeable wall tones may be found in pale luminous green, aqua, pink, delicate yellow. Dark colored bedrooms may be wanted by late-risers. Bedrooms can have strong contrasts because the need for a soft and uniform seeing condition is not as urgent.

In bathrooms, pink and coral are difficult colors to excel. Such interiors are usually small, and wall reflections will make the flesh radiant and roseate. One of the best cool colors is turquoise, which complements the tint of human complexion.

In kitchens, color variety is practical. Time seems to pass more quickly where there is much visual interest. Simple red, yellow, blue, and white are

good. Technical practice would prescribe the use of colored mats and counters for food preparation in order to lessen the glare of white. Red, however, should be avoided in preference to blue, green, or gray for work surfaces.

Recreation areas may also take bright colors and great variety.

Coming Trends

There is much in color that is both personal and impersonal. Functional color involves factors which are more or less objective and measurable and which have to do with good visibility and the proper functioning of the human organism, spiritual and esthetic qualities aside. Psychodécor is the intimate

The translucent wall in the rear of the garden is of blue-green alsynite. The neutral colors of the floor and the ceiling set off the red trellis beams, green and yellow curtains, and red cushions. Raphael Soriano, architect.

Applebaum house, Long Island, New York. Nemeny & Geller, architects. A feeling of spaciousness is emphasized by the use of simple colors and uncluttered surfaces. (Ezra Stoller photograph.)

Dupree house, Akron, Ohio. Robert Little, architect. A kitchen that anticipates the future with its unusual arrangement and variety of fixtures, appliances, and cabinets. (Lionel Freedman photograph.)

Subtle variations in color, making full use of the natural appearance of the materials, distinguish this Case Study house by Craig Ellwood. The entrance hall, shown on the facing page, leads one into the rest of the house by skillful use of light. (Marvin Rand photograph.)

study, the personal one in which psychic qualities are regarded. Here, perhaps, is where the art of interior design will find its greatest incentive and where most progress will be made.

In a broad sense, the world becomes more socialized with time. Large class differences are lessened. Science, government, art, and architecture seek more democratic expressions. The former chasm between luxury and squalor is narrowed and leveled off. Large scale housing, community centers in place of awkward monuments, decentralized industrial areas, the even greater concentration of women in industry — all these trends offer wider uses for color.

Consider an average community and all the places in which color may play a significant role. Its public buildings, city halls, court houses, municipal buildings; its health centers, recreational areas; its trucks and equipment; its hospitals, schools, churches; its commercial establishments and stores; its factories and office buildings; its homes and farms — all these are places in which color may serve useful as well as attractive ends.

Vanity alone seems rather minor. New technicians in color are needed with new training. Surely the educational process will include not only the art studio but the laboratory of the lighting engineer, the ophthalmologist and authority in vision, the psychologist and psychiatrist. The art and science of color should work for achievements that will advance the best causes and desires of a modern age.

14

Traditional Home

Interiors

The most personal of all uses of color is in the home. And here, unfortunately, is where human taste is often at its worst. While a home should by all means express the personality of its occupants, the inexperienced eye is likely to misjudge colors, to get them too vivid, to harmonize them too awkwardly.

If the interior designer and decorator may be criticized, he may be charged with two simple faults. First, he may create a very original environment for very unoriginal people, making the home a showplace in which the occupants seem apart, like visitors at a store or museum. Second, he may try too hard to achieve the anomalous, often accomplishing little more than a sterile bleakness or a mess of fussy ambiguities; he may seek temporary values that reflect a passing style, and he may be oblivious to the emotional and temperamental needs of his client.

Color Traditions

In ancient times color expression was vigorous. It became gaudy and baroque during the Renaissance, restrained and austere during the Reformation, sophisticated in the days before the French Revolution, classical during Greek and Roman revivals, grandiose during the Victorian era, and now lucid and frank in these days of realism.

The Egyptians, who appear to have started everything, held a strong liking for elementary hues, generally arranged in triads: red, yellow, blue; red, blue, white; deep red, soft yellow, blue; deep blue, light blue, white; blue, buff, black.

In Asia Minor, the palette of the decoration (in temples, not homes) showed great advancement due to more versatile materials such as ceramics. Assyrian tiles had such color schemes as these:

Blue-green, yellow-green, orange, brown, and white.
Blue, yellow, white, deep red, and black.
Blue, deep yellow, pale yellow, and white.
Pale yellow, green, blue, red, gold, black, and white.
Black, yellow, green, red, blue, and white.
Green, blue-green, yellow, white, deep red, and black.

Textiles were usually patterned and generously decorated, with colored fringes and bands.

In the Orient, red, yellow, and gold predominated. Expression was direct and meaningful. And the same applied to the Oriental rug. George Birdwood wrote: "Whatever their type of ornamentation may be, a deep and complicated symbolism, originating in Babylonia and possibly India, pervades every denomination of Oriental carpets. . . . Every color used has its significance." And again: "The very irregularities, either in drawing or coloring. . . are seldom accidental, the usual deliberate intention being to avert the evil eye and insure good luck."

The Greeks also used simple hues such as red, yellow, blue, and black, this combination being the common palette of the fresco painter. Well preserved textiles dating back to the fifth century B. C. show traces of vivid pigment — red with black figures, gold with blue, and Tyrian purple.

Democritus tells of fabrics in blue-violet, purple, and saffron, patterned and trimmed with borders. Others were in bright green, purple, and white; dark violet, light violet, or hyacinth color; bright red and sea green. Many were embellished with gold tinsel.

In Rome the vigorous palette was as much a part of interior decoration as it was of all the arts and crafts. Textiles were usually made of wool and often dyed blue or red. There are excellent records of Pompeian interiors. Many of these were solidly painted in black, vermilion, clear blue, and terra cotta and decorated with flowers, figures, animals, and elaborate paintings out of mythology.

Then came the Dark Ages and the prelude of the Gothic, with the drab interior and the luminous art of stained glass contrasted side by side — one ashen, the other brilliant with the luster of precious stones, red and blue predominating.

Renaissance Colors

In the Renaissance an eloquence in color rivaled the eloquence of Italian sculpture and painting. All this was supposed to glorify a rebirth of classical pagan ideals. Art and color reached one of the most garish and spectacular periods in all its history.

Most people are familiar with Renaissance styles, the flourish of elaborate decoration and ornament, the use of architecture to set off sculpture and to frame painting. The color sense was sophisticated, with the sky the limit. Florentine decoration was rich with yellow, yellow-orange, blue-green, and light slate blues. Sixteenth and seventeenth century brocades had such color schemes as yellow-green ornaments on deep violet; light olive green on dark blue; harmonies that were subtle and with a delicacy unknown in former ages.

These old Italian color schemes are properly termed exquisite. They bear listing. Here are a few notations copied from Renaissance brocades. They were developed by men highly sensitive and skilled in color choice.

Purple and yellowish green ornaments on blue-violet ground; outlines in gold.

Dull crimson, pale blue, and yellow ornaments on dark gray ground.

Pale yellow-green ornaments on deep amber ground.

Light yellow-green and dark blue-green ornaments on deep crimson ground.

Pale blue-green ornaments on dark gray-blue ground, with touches of white and gold.

Emerald green and dull orange ornaments on dark gray-green ground; outlines in gold.

Period Styles

Practically all period styles date back to either classical or Renaissance traditions.

The French periods, notably Louis XV, are sumptuous, enthusiastically Renaissance, and luxurious with brilliant and exclusive hues: light blues,

Venetian bedroom of the Renaissance period. The colors are rich and sophisticated to match the complexity of design. Courtesy of Metropolitan Museum of Art.

Interior of the Louis XV period. A rich use of natural wood and marble, offset by gold and uncommon tones of rose, green, and purple, mark this elaborate style of decoration. Courtesy of Metropolitan Museum of Art.

View of kitchen in early 17th century American home. Note use of natural materials. Color, where used, was fashioned of simple pigments and dyes. Courtesy of Metropolitan Museum of Art.

View of 18th century American interior. In upper class homes, wall colors were usually muted but tastefully contrasted with multicolor effects in wallpaper, fabrics, and carpeting. Courtesy of Metropolitan Museum of Art.

violets, odd greens, purples, grays, gold — probably through the influence of Madame de Pompadour, who favored subtlety in colors.

The Louis XVI style goes back to simpler classical ideals, both in design and color. Under the influence of Marie Antoinette, colors were delicate and affected. Under the influence of the eminent painter David, there was extreme severity and formality.

French Empire was to a large extent inspired by Napoleon's visits to Italy. Napoleon showed preference for red, green, white, and gold, Josephine for the more delicate tints of blue, violet, purple, and tan.

The English periods are more temperate. The Georgian style is largely Roman and Pompeian, though more reserved. The Adam style is directly Pompeian. Josiah Wedgwood's classical Greek ceramics are simple in color, severe, and pure in tradition. Adam, however, introduced less primary hues — soft blue, pale yellow, lilac, delicate gray, blue-green, yellow-green, and pink.

The craftsmanship of Chippendale, Hepplewhite, and Sheraton also emphasized the subtle beauty of wood tones, which became definitely tied in with interior schemes.

Finally, the Victorian style was flamboyant. Colors were generally low keyed — brown, purplish red, deep green. The wide use of purples and magentas has distinguished the era as the Mauve Decade.

Native American Traditions

In pre-revolutionary America, colors were decidedly English in quality. In the restorations at Williamsburg a carefully recorded palette shows a few rich colors such as deep red, Chinese red, deep green, and yellow. For the most part, however, there was an appreciation for soft tones of warm green, tan, medium gray, pale green, blue-green, and rose. The taste in general was aristocratic and refined, but with a liberal tolerance for much color variety.

Wealthy Americans of the Colonial period copied their styles from England. The results may be seen today in preserved or restored Colonial buildings at Mount Vernon and Monticello. The humble farmer or craftsman, however, was far less pretentious. His furniture, for instance, although disdained by the rich Tory, had a simple and functional beauty which has impressed Americans —and the world — right down the generations to the present. Neat wood houses were frequently painted in a deep red hue called Spanish brown. This was made from a pigment dug out of the earth. It was nearly always used for the priming coat on the exterior of a house and was

often the sole paint applied. In 1769 John Gore of Boston advertised: "Very good red, black, yellow paints, the produce and manufacture of North America."

For interiors, blues and greens were favorites, often with the green made olive or the blue grayed by the addition of black. Vivid hues were found on spattered floors, plastered walls, and woodwork. White, gray, pearly tones, and stone shades seemed to have been favored for meeting houses.

Today white is overemphasized in Colonial revivals, although it did have quite a vogue in the late eighteenth century. The colonist usually preferred deeper and more intense hues. These elementary colors they applied with a simplicity and candor that well fitted their architecture.

Antebellum Days

Among the wealthier planters of the South, most of the aristocratic traditions from Colonial America were preserved. Although New England Yankees, venturesome souls who went west into Kentucky, Ohio, and Michigan, lived a modest and frugal existence (with simple need for color), the South was able to maintain its luxuries. Colonial wallpapers based on classical designs, plus realistically colored floral forms, had an enduring rage. The gamut of hue ranged from soft grays and tans to brilliant red embellishments. Light woodwork was favored.

This indulgence later melted into the Victorian flair for color and became more or less confused with it. Today, in truth, Southern decoration looks Victorian and probably is.

Bedroom in the home of John D. Rockefeller, about 1885. Restored by Museum of the City of New York. Here the Victorian style is at its sumptuous height, with practically every color of the spectrum represented. (Gottscho-Schleisner photograph.)

Recent Trends

National trends have undergone slow but steady change over the years. A generation ago, green, rust, and some purple were in greatest demand. Shortly before World War II this preference had shifted to rose and blue. Today America is back to green again, this time without the rust and the purple. Desired hues are gray and beige, with some flesh tones and "shocking" pink, much chartreuse and yellow, and lesser amounts of turquoise, dull blue, brown, and white.

Although these schemes change slowly, there are certain universal values in color which seem to prevail at any time. One of these is a liking for pale wall colors as against deep ones. Another is a preference for deep colors in draperies — burgundy, navy, dark green. Still again, the simpler hues — ivory, pale green, pale blue, yellow, pink, tan — are in demand at all times and appear to hold their popularity, whereas other and higher style trends come and go. This bears out research by psychologists in which it is found that where a choice is offered, (a) simple colors (red, blue, green) are preferred over intermediate hues (yellow-green, blue-green, violet, and purple), (b) pure colors are preferred as against grayish ones, and (c) light colors are preferred over deep ones.

Functionally considered, the pale colors and elementary ones are good choices for facilities devoted to factory workers, office employees, school children, and hospital patients. Esthetically, however, the decorator will find more unusual appeal in colors which depart from the conventional.

The Parthenon restored. Natural marble was painted with a simple palette of ivory, red, yellow, green, and blue. This treatment was more symbolic than realistic. Courtesy of Metropolitan Museum of Art.

Interior of Parthenon restored. In the original state, the effigy of Athena was gilded, and the sculpture and ornamentation were richly hued throughout. Courtesy of Metropolitan Museum of Art.

15

The Story of

Color in

Architecture

Little has been written on the history of color in architecture. The few studies available seem to be based more on personal deductions than on a scholarly understanding of the mind and spirit of ancient man. The surviving ruins of temple and tomb have been pieced together and conclusions drawn which have seldom dealt also with the scarce literary records of early days. In many costly and beautifully illustrated tomes on ancient architecture, the text is usually brief and concerned for the most part with what the compiler of the book thought or deduced for himself.

It is known, for example, that the Western world knew little if anything of the use of color in classical Greek architecture until the eighteenth century! And when the fact was discovered, few writers were able to explain it understandably.

However, there were definite reasons for color in early architecture, reasons that involved symbolism and mythology. Indeed, the early architect seldom expressed his own feelings. Rather, he complied with the traditions of his day and he took his instructions from religious leaders who told him more or less precisely what he was to do.

Misconceptions of Color

Books on architecture frequently refer to the works of Rhys Carpenter and Lisle March Phillips on the esthetic basis of ancient art. If the author may be forgiven, he wishes to take exception to a number of misconceptions

153

which he feels have arisen and which are still today referred to in architectural books and passed on to students in colleges and universities.

For example, Phillips surveyed the art of former times and came to the conclusion that, "Form has dominated art whenever and wherever the intellectual faculty was dominant in life; color has dominated art whenever and wherever the emotional faculty has dominated life." The West was said to have form and science, while the East had color and mysticism. There is more conjecture than fact in this observation, for the equanimity of the Eastern mind is one of mental and intellectual poise, quite in contrast with the impulsiveness and emotional instability of the Westerner. Phillips, however, came to this strange conclusion: "It seems natural that the Western temperament, intellectual rather than sensuous, should excel in form rather than color; while the Eastern, sensuous rather than intellectual, should excel in color rather than form."

It can be seriously questioned if the Brahman or Buddhist was less intellectual than the Frenchman or Englishman, and if Westerners were less sensuous than Easterners. Such an error of judgment might readily follow a perusal of ancient art forms which did not at the same time take ancient philosophy into account. Phillips concludes, "What always distinguishes Oriental color is its own glow and richness, apart from definite meanings or explanatory purposes attaching to it." This is a complete reversal of fact. It is the Westerner who has used color without meaning, a mere decorative luxury in design. The Easterner has always had purposes in mind: the invocation of spirits, the execration of demons, the use of symbols to express his philosophy and religion. He has seldom been without profundity in the use of color.

The Ancient Mind

The beauty of Egyptian, Chaldean, and Greek art arose not out of esthetics alone but out of religion and superstition. Art was functional and practical in that it was symbolic. The Egyptians used it to "deny the physical evidence of death." The *ziggurats* of Babylon were veritable charts of mysticism in architecture. The palaces of China were painstakingly designed to emblem the five elements, two essences, and ultimate principle of the universe. The early sculpture of Greece was not abstract in conception but used to personify gods and mortals.

The evidence of history pretty well defeats the attempt to speak of creative art in the modern sense. Why was the palette always simple: red, yellow, green, blue, purple, white, black? How could the Greek mind, so sensitive to form, to balance and the harmony of line and mass, make so little effort to be subtle with hue? Beechey very aptly remarks, "We observe that the practice we allude to does not appear . . . to be the result of any occasional caprice or fancy, but of a generally established system; for the colors of the several parts do not seem to have materially varied in any two instances with which we are acquainted . . . We can scarcely doubt that one particular color was appropriated by general consent or practice to each of the several parts of the buildings."

If the Greeks or any civilized men before them were trying to express highly personal feelings, how may one account for this apparently matter-of-fact and commonplace use of the spectrum? The answer must be that the ancient artist had definite reasons for color just as he had sound ideas about architecture. He was a humble votary who gave himself not to the whims of his own individuality but to the social and religious consciousness of his people. He was not a creator in the modern sense, but an interpreter. He did not seek to inspire men with *his* sense of beauty, but to follow dictates and principles set before him by others.

Symbolism and Mythology

When one realizes that practically every surviving archaeological record of ancient times is a temple or tomb — not an office building, state capitol, library, museum, school, or home — one may appreciate that religious thought and expression ruled the day.

In religion, man included his philosophy and science. The great principles of nature and the vital forces of the universe were personified by gods and goddesses. Religion held sway not only over the spirit of man (as today) but also over his mind and every institution of government. The foremost brains of antiquity — teachers, scientists, philosophers, priests, physicians — were the mystics. They guided the empire, regulated the affairs of war and peace, commerce and industry, and formed the intelligence and culture of nations.

The sun was the principle of good, master of sky and earth, sustaining all life and controlling the universe. To the Egyptian it was Osiris. To the Persian it was Mithras. To the Hindu it was Brahma. To the Chaldean it was Bel. To the Greek it was Adonis and Apollo. God was the supreme deity associated with light. His emanations gave hue to the rainbow. They pervaded all space, put breath and spirit into the body of man. The golden ornaments of priests and the crowns of kings referred to the sun. Red, yellow, green, blue, purple were a part of these emanations, each significant, each emblematic of divine forces.

In Egypt yellow and gold were tokens of the sun. The color of man was red. Green represented the eternity of nature. Purple was the hue of earth. Blue, like the heavens, was sacred to justice. It was worn on the breastplates of Egyptian priests to indicate the holiness of their judgments.

Osiris, the father of the Egyptian trinity, was green. His son Horus was white. Set, the deity of evil, was black. Shu, who separated earth from sky, was red. Amen, the god of life and reproduction, was blue.

Time was addressed as the "everlasting green one." The races of man were four in number — red for the Egyptians, yellow for the Asiatics, white for the peoples of the north, black for the Negro. In the ritualism of death, amulets and colors buried in the tomb of the deceased brought security until the time of resurrection. A green stone performed "the opening of the mouth," restoring speech to the corpse. The red *Tjet* gave the virtue of the blood of Isis. The red *Ab*, or heart amulet, preserved the soul of the physical body. The golden *Udjat* afforded health and protection. The red *Nefer* brought happiness and fortune. The brownish *Sma* caused breath to return.

All these involved significant works of art that glisten today in the glass cases of museums. Men in the time of Egypt were obviously not catering

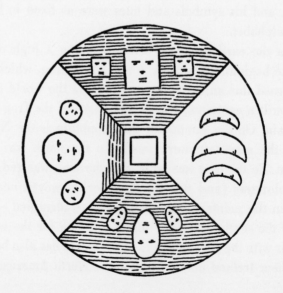

Sumur Mountain, an ancient Mongolian conception of the universe as a pyramid having a different hue on each side with heaven at the apex.

to vanity nor indulging themselves in mere artistic expression. Egyptian amulets, vignettes, coffin decorations, the rubrics of manuscripts, temples, sculptural ornaments, painting — all had purposes. They were designed to symbolize the Mysteries, to invoke the favor of the gods, to seek victory over nature, affliction, plague, drought, and death, to serve life first, last, and always. Where the modern artist speaks of the intrinsic beauty of color, its ability to thrill the emotions through the eye, the Egyptian was primarily concerned with a language of color that was precise rather than vague in its meaning.

Oriental Symbolism

In the Orient this same use of color prevailed. Gods were identified by hues. In India Brahma was yellow; Siva the destroyer was black. Yellow was likewise sacred to Buddha and to Confucius. Green was sacred to Mohammed and is still worn in the turban of the Moslem who has made a pilgrimage to Mecca.

Architecturally, however, most color symbolism came from the study of astrology. This science originated in Chaldee and was practiced two thousand years before the birth of Christ. Great temples were dedicated to the gods of the heavens and designated in color to symbolize the seven planets.

Throughout Asia color, architecture, and design answered to the Mysteries. Everything had meaning. Art was created out of belief. There were few abstractions as today, murals that attempt to spiritualize commerce, history, and what not through the emotional implications of hue. The Oriental had a story to tell, and his symbols and hues were as fixed in his mind as the letters of the alphabet.

In Mongolia the earth was conceived as being a high mountain called Sumur. "In the beginning was only water and a frog, which gazed into the water. God turned this animal over and created the world on its belly. On each foot he built a continent, but on the navel of the frog he founded the Sumur Mountain. On the summit of this mountain is the North Star." The four sides of the mountain were hued. To the north was yellow. To the south was blue. To the east was white. To the west was red.

In China color was (and still is) inextricably woven into the culture of the race. Again the points of the compass were identified — black for the north, red for the south, green for the east, white for the west. (This association of color with the four quarters of the world has also been found in the culture of ancient Ireland and the Indians of North America.)

To the Chinese the primary colors were five in number, red, yellow, black, white, green (and blue). These hues were related to the five Chinese elements, fire, metal, wood, earth, and water, to the five happinesses, the five virtues, the five vices, the five precepts of faith.

Dynasties were known by hues, brown for the Sung Dynasty, green for the Ming, yellow for the Ch'ing. The emperor wore blue when he worshipped the sky, yellow when he worshipped the earth. He signed all edicts with vermilion ink. His officials wore colored buttons atop their caps to distinguish their rank. His grandchildren rode in purple sedans, his higher officials in blue, his lower officials in green.

In the Chinese theater the sacred person was indicated by a red face; the face of the boor was black, the villain white. These colors were as unmistakably clear in meaning as the black mustaches and blond curls of performers in a Victorian melodrama. They were understood by all, serf and king. To bless the emperor the priest chanted, "These white jewels are a prognostic of the great august white hairs to which your Majesty will reach. The red jewels are the august, healthful, ruddy countenance, and the green jewels are the harmonious fitness which your Majesty will establish far and wide."

Occidental Symbolism

Chinese, Hindu, Chaldean, and Egyptian learning was the basis of Greek and Roman culture. Naturally the color traditions of these earlier civilizations crossed the Hellespont to dwell on the continent north of the Mediterranean. The old gods were given new names. Athena, wise in the arts of peace and war, was adorned with a yellow robe. Red was sacred to Ceres and to Dionysus. Pythagoras wrote of the two virgins of the temple, one veiled in a white robe, the other bedecked with the jewels of earthly treasures. A white robe symbolized purity, a red robe sacrifice and love, a blue robe altruism and integrity. When acting the Odyssey, the Greeks wore purple to symbolize the sea-wanderings of Ulysses. For the Iliad they wore scarlet in reference to the bloody battles of the poem.

Later in Rome purple became the imperial color, Caesar wearing it to personify Jupiter.

Sculpture in Greece comprised the fashioning of effigies, gods and goddesses who lived and breathed and even vanished from one place to appear in another. One writer describes a freshly unearthed pediment: "Flesh, reddish in tone; globe of eyes yellow, iris green, with a hole in the center filled with black; black outlines to eyebrows and eyelids; hair and beard bright blue at the time of excavation, which disintegrated later to a greenish tone; circle of brown around the nipples."

But the color art of Greece has not been well preserved because of deterioration. Much of it was lost for centuries, during which artists and architects devoted themselves to the adoration of form and gave rebirth to classic styles in which color was sadly missing. Greek artists, however, gave symbolism to color just as did the savants of former times. Mythology told of the four ages of man, gold, silver, copper, and iron. The science of the universe as comprised of four elements, earth, fire, water, and air, led to the theory of Pythagoras that earth-particles were cubical, fire-particals tetrahedral, water-particles icosahedral, air-particles octahedral. The fifth solid, a dodecahedron symbolized the ether. The sphere, perfect among all symmetrical solids, was reserved for the deity.

And once again colors were significantly applied, blue to symbolize earth, red for fire, green for water, and yellow for air. (Other designations were given later. Josephus in the first century spoke of white earth, red fire, purple water, blue air. Da Vinci in the fifteenth century related yellow to earth, red to fire, green to water, and blue to air.) Man himself was composed of colors and elements, his flesh and bone of blueness and earth, his bodily heat of redness and fire, his blood and fluids of greenness and water, the gases within him of yellowness and air.

Other Traditions

One may trace the same august respect for color among other races throughout the world. The Druids of England used green, blue, and white in their rituals. In some civilizations human beings were sacrificed in a red temple draped with red hangings. The elements were controlled through incantations and rites that involved colors. The ceremonies of birth, circumcision, puberty, marriage, death were rich in color associations. Amulets, charms, and hues brought protection over the household, thwarted the evil eye, drove away disease.

As paganism died in Western countries, to be replaced by Christianity, color began to lose its importance. Yet not entirely. Cabalism spoke of a trinity of blue, yellow, and red. The Egyptian trinity of Osiris, Isis, and Horus, the Hindu trinity of Brahma, Vishnu, and Siva, the philosophic notion of life, birth, and death, of past, present, and future, of dawn, day, and dusk, gave way to a new theology. Now there was God the Father, Creator of the

The Tabernacle in the Wilderness. Described in the Bible, this edifice was colored in accordance with prescribed ritual, the chief hue being blue.

world, whose hue was blue to symbolize heaven and the spirt of man. God the Son was radiant in the fullness of day; His hue was yellow, the symbol of earth and the mind of man. God the Holy Ghost was the setting sun; His hue was red, the symbol of hell and the body of man.

The mystic struggled to preserve color traditions. He pointed to numerous references in the Bible, visions of the Lord, laws for the construction of the Tabernacle. The Tablets of the Law given to Moses had been fashioned of divine sapphire. A red carbuncle had shone from the prow of Noah's Ark. The Holy Grail had been green. St. John had spoken of the New Jerusalem and its twelve foundations garnished with twelve different hues and jewels. He had told of four horses, one white, one red, one black, one pale, of the woman arrayed in purple and scarlet.

There was thought to be symbolism in all this, a key to the mysteries of life. But the Church turned from paganism, and the mystic was vanquished.

Yet his fervor did not pass entirely. It was revived by the alchemist and in medieval times glowed once more — black, the darkness and beginning of all things; white, the light of creation; red and gold, the glory of the sun. Alchemy influenced the early Gothic architect, and like the craftsman of old he used color to symbolic purpose. But his iniquity was discovered and his works covered with whitewash. In 1652 one Elias Ashmole wrote of such an event — the destruction of an alchemical design in color on an arched wall in Westminster Abbey. "Notwithstanding it has pleased some, to wash the *Originall* over with a *Plasterer's* whited *Brush.*"

Architecture in Egypt and Asia Minor

To go back again, Egyptian color in architecture and decoration was simple, the red hue of man, the purple of earth, the yellow of the sun, the green of nature, the blue of divine truth. There are still vestiges of red pigment on the face of the Sphinx. The chambers of the Great Pyramid, however, far older, are faded and indicate but an elemental symbolism. Generally the ceilings of tombs and temples were blue and embellished with pictures of the constellations. The floors were green and blue like the meadows of the Nile.

The four races of man according to the ancient Egyptians, each race having a color symbol.

RED   YELLOW   BLACK   WHITE

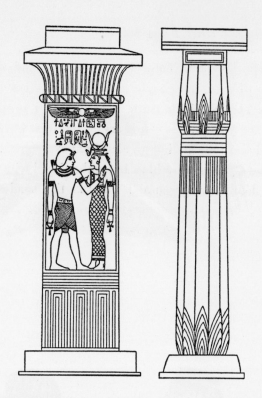

Sketches from Karnak. Egyptian sculpture was colorfully decorated in red, gold, green, and blue.

The brilliant color at Karnak featured the same red, yellow, green, blue that was part of the Egyptian Mysteries. Limestone, sandstone, granite, flinty diorite, the materials of the time, were glazed and painted to conform to the dictates of religion. The king wore a high white crown to symbolize his dominion over upper Egypt, and his treasury here was called the "White House." A flat red crown proclaimed his mastery over lower Egypt and the treasury of the "Red House."

As in Egypt, so also in Mesopotamia and Asia. Here the study of astrology led to a symbolism for color that dominated all architecture. Woolley in a joint expedition of the British Museum and the Museum of Pennsylvania unearthed the ancient *ziggurat*, the "Mountain of God," at Ur between Bagdad and the Persian Gulf, one of the oldest buildings in the world.

The tower measured about 200 feet in length, 150 feet in width, and was originally about 70 feet high. It was built in four stages, a great solid mass of brickwork. At the top was the square shrine of Nannar, the Moon-God. Woolley found an absence of straight lines. Horizontal planes bulged out-

The Mountain of God at Ur near Bagdad, one of the oldest known buildings. It was built in four stages and colored in black, blue, red, and gold.

ward, vertical planes were slightly convex — a subtlety once thought to be of Greek origin and quite evident in the Parthenon.

The lowest stage of this tower was black, the uppermost red. The shrine was covered with blue glazed tile, the roof with gilded metal. Woolley writes, "These colors had their mystical significance and stood for the various divisions of the universe, the dark underworld, the habitable earth, the heavens and the sun."

More pretentious *ziggurats* have been unearthed. In the fifth century B. C., Herodotus wrote of Ecbatana. "The Medes built the city now called Ecbatana, the walls of which are of great size and strength, rising in circles one within the other. The plan of the place is, that each of the walls should out-top the one beyond it by the battlements. The nature of the ground, which is a gentle hill, favors this arrangement in some degree, but it was mainly effected by art. The number of the circles is seven, the royal palace and the treasuries standing within the last. The circuit of the outer wall is very nearly the same with that of Athens. Of this wall the battlements are white, of the next black, of the third scarlet, of the fourth blue, of the fifth orange; all these are colored with paint. The two last have their battlements coated respectively with silver and gold. All these fortifications Deioces had caused to be raised for himself and his own palace."

Herodotus to all indications referred to the great temple of Nebuchadnezzar at Barsippa, the Birs Nimroud. Uncovered in modern times, its bricks bear the stamp of the Babylonian monarch who apparently rebuilt it in the seventh century B. C. It was 272 feet square at its base and rose in seven stages, each stage being set back away from a central point. Of this building Fergusson wrote, "This temple, as we know from the decipherment of the cylinders which were found on its angles, was dedicated to the seven planets or heavenly spheres, and we find it consequently adorned with the colors of each. The lower, which was also richly paneled, was black, the color of Saturn; the next, orange, the color of Jupiter; the third, red, emblematic of Mars; the fourth, yellow, belonging to the sun; the fifth and sixth, green and blue respectively, as dedicated to Venus and Mercury, and the upper probably white, that being the color belonging to the moon, whose place in the Chaldean system would be uppermost."

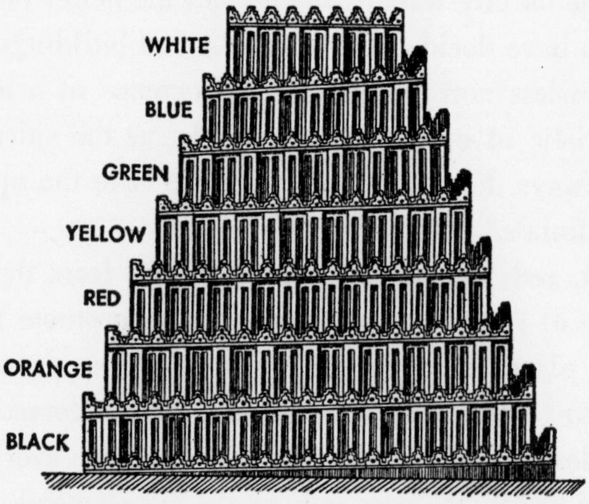

The Temple of Nebuchadnezzar at Barsippa. This typical "Tower of Babel," like all others, was richly colored with symbolic hues. After Fergusson.

WHITE
BLUE
GREEN
YELLOW
RED
ORANGE
BLACK

Chinese Architecture

In China like conventions were followed. In the humble dwelling, homes of more than two stories were avoided. In his *Outlines of Chinese Symbolism,* Williams writes, "Height is also limited by the belief that good spirits soar through the air at a height of 100 feet, a restriction of moment only in great temples and other buildings on city walls. Climate and the belief that good spirits blow from the south have decided the orientation of buildings with a southern aspect and windowless north walls. The abhorrence of a tortuous path, which is a characteristic of evil spirits, has given us the spirit walls which define so many gateways. For the same reason we have the upcurved roof edge with its dragon finials."

When a home was built, red firecrackers were exploded from the upper beam of the roof. A piece of red cloth was suspended to promote felicity. Green pine branches were placed atop the scaffolding to deceive wandering evil spirits and led them to believe they were passing over a forest.

In the palaces and temples of China one finds color symbolism everywhere. As in the Forbidden City of Peking the hues emblem the five elements, virtues, vices, etc. Red shows as the positive essence, the heavenly and masculine principle. Yellow shows as the negative essence, the earthly and feminine principle. Thus the walls of Peking are red, symbolic of the south, the sun, happiness. The roofs are yellow, symbolic of the earth.

Sketch of Chinese temple. There was a full use of red and gold, each having a definite significance.

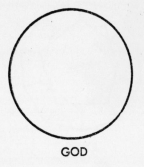

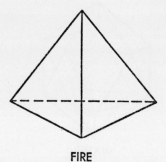

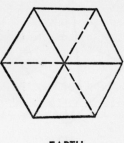

GOD   FIRE   EARTH

Greek Architecture

Such roads lead to Greece. The choice of hues remains very much the same — red, yellow, green, blue. Even in sculpture, where the Greek far surpassed the artists of other nations, he did not venture to extend the palette. Frederik Poulsen describes Greek coloring: "When the reliefs were discovered, they were richly painted, and still the colors have not all faded. As was indicated in the treatment of the metopes of the Sicyonian Treasury, the background was blue. The figures are treated in blue, green, and red, the last color in two shades, light red and golden-red. The clothes are red with blue borders, while the colors are changed when two or more articles of clothing or armor are worn. The helmets are blue, with red ornamental stripes on the edges, to pick them out from the blue background; the last features remind one of the little red nimbus which in red-figured vases divides the dark hair of the figures from the dark ground. The outsides of the shields are alternately blue and red, their insides red, with a narrow colorless border along the edge, a color scheme answering exactly to that of figures on the Aeginetan pediment. The bodies of Cybele's lions are colorless, but the manes, harness, and yoke are red. The tails and manes of the horses are red, or where several are seen close together, alternately red and blue."

It was because of such reports that Rodin was said to have struck his breast and shouted, "I feel it here that these were never colored."

But colored they were, all Greek sculpture and all Greek architecture! Yet the expression was better and showed a finer respect for mass and delineation.

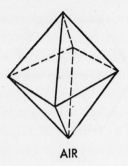
AIR

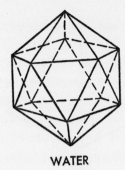
WATER

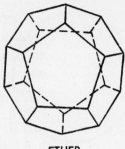
ETHER

Solon has given an excellent account of Greek method, the struggle for symmetry and balance. Color was restricted mainly to the superstructure of buildings. There was little or no color in retaining walls, in the peristyle, the column shaft or base, except the ivory tint which the Greek seemed to prefer to white marble.

The solids of Pythagoras symbolizing the elements, each identified by hue.

In the Doric style red and blue were introduced in the capital. The Ionic capital frequently had gold, red, and blue. Examples of Corinthian capitals, which are rare, show gold to be preferred.

Generally the treatment was as follows:

The architrave was not colored.
The taenia was usually red.
The triglyph was dark blue or black.
The corona was uncolored.
The cyma was the most ornate of all moldings, black, red, white being
   commonly used.
The mutules were dark blue or black.
The roof tiles were often terra cotta or marble.
The full palette was employed in architectural sculpture.

Modern artists have often wondered at the Greek for covering wood, metal, and the purest of marbles with pigment. Why did he, blessed by the rarest sense of form in all history, apply a thick coating over virgin materials? How could he let an encaustic painter touch up his work as one might a doll?

There is but one satisfactory answer. Sculpture and architecture were not matters of "art" in the modern sense. They were not based on individualism, on soulful expression, the communion of man with his own ego. They arose out of the common need of craftsmen to glorify what all people believed. Hues were formalized because they were part of religion, tokens of eternal principles. To change the Greek palette would be to change science, mythology, and Hellenic wisdom. Nothing like this occurred to artist or architect. Color had functions to perform. A man could not wander apart in his own mind; he must comply with religious dictates and traditions.

The Decline of Color

As Greek architecture emigrated to Rome, the use of color declined. The Romans, in truth, erected buildings of white marble and left them uncoated with wax or pigment. Here was the beginning of an austerity that was to continue down through the centuries.

In the Byzantine style there was a return to more luxury, though without a definite symbolism. St. Sophia's at Constantinople was built with colorful marble in red, green, blue, black. Portals were covered with gold leaf. Jewels and pearls were woven into curtains. These were carved cedar, amber, ivory, mosaic, cast metal. The architecture and the application of color influenced certain later Christian churches and also, indirectly, the mosques of Islam, the Alhambra, and Alcazar.

With the growth of the Gothic style in the Middle Ages the more formal and symbolic qualities of ancient times were replaced by naturalistic tendencies. As in Byzantium, color was a stimulus to emotion, not a definition of universal principles.

James Ward has written that the early buildings and monuments of France were colored inside as well as outside. Realistic paintings and decorations were common. The façade of Notre Dame still bears traces of such art. There was much gilding. Describing the great cathedral Ward writes, "The coloring occurred principally on the moldings, columns, sculptured ornaments and figure work. The outside coloring was much more vivid than the inside work. There were bright reds, crude greens, orange, yellow ochre, blacks and pure whites, but rarely blues, outside, the brilliancy of light allowing a harshness of coloring that would not be tolerable under the diffused light of the interior. The large gables of the transept also bear traces of old painting. There is also evidence that the greater portion of similar edifices of the thirteenth, fourteenth and fifteenth centuries, in France, were decorated in color." And the same was true in Italy, Spain, Germany, England.

The Renaissance

Then came the Renaissance, which Victor Hugo once described as "that setting sun all Europe mistook for dawn." The art of color was now in serious decline.

Ralph Adams Cram in his introduction to Solon's *Polychromy* observes, "The complete loss of color out of architecture is one of the curious phenomena of the Renaissance, casting its drab shadow in lengthening lines and ever-increasing gloom over the art of building in modern times." The old order of art passed quickly into oblivion. Where the ancient craftsman had been humbly a part of society, deferring to traditions, customs, and the accepted principles of faith, the new artist walked apart from men. Self-expression, originality, egocentricity prevailed.

The introduction of oil painting drew emphasis to the subtleties of light and shade. Color used to model shape. Many architects came from the ranks of painters, men like Giotto, Michaelangelo, Raphael, Alberti, Vasari. Some of them even applied the principles of chiaroscuro (light and shade) to building design. They were attracted to realism and often considered architecture little more than a stage-setting for painting.

Soon after came the use of fancy marbles, mosaics, burnished gold-leaf, colored brick, terra cotta. The art of color was turned from symbolism to abstract and purely impersonal theories of color arrangement, often lavish. And still later the Reformation was to disdain even this and to leave records of drab and gray sterility.

The Modern Era

Le Corbusier once wrote, "The lesson of Rome is for wise men, for those who know and can appreciate, who can resist and can verify. Rome is the damnation of the half-educated. To send architectural students to Rome is to cripple them for life."

What is the modern significance of color? With what are modern theories of color concerned? From the Renaissance to the present — about 500 years — men have looked at the spectrum as a thing apart from life, a delight to the eye, a balm to the emotions, useful to make architecture pleasing to the senses. Yet from Memphis to the Renaissance — over 4,000 years! — color had meaning and symbolism. Men understood it and worshipped it because they assigned definitions to it.

Color has had revivals every now and then since St. Peter's. Charles

Garnier, who built the Paris Opera House in 1871 said, "The grounds of the cornices will shine with eternal colors, the piers will be enriched with sparkling panels, gilded friezes will run along the buildings. The monuments will be clothed with marbles and enamels, and mosaics will make all love movement and color."

But visions of this sort have been of little avail. Garnier himself used color (and design) badly. One cannot build art out of dreams alone. Some modern architects have instinctively felt the magic of the rainbow, the profound love expressed for it by the world at large. And in the twentieth century color has gradually crept back, humbly at first in hamburger stand and filling station. In the World's Fairs of Chicago and New York color has been used freely and boldly, but with little effect on architectural trends. A few large buildings have been designed in glazed terra cotta and facing tile. Yet here once again, no great movement toward color is to be noted. The austerity of the Roman and Gothic styles continues to prevail.

However, acceptance of color becomes more universal with time. It stands a good chance of catching on yet, as a general element in architecture rather than as an experimental exception. If color is to return, what will be done with it?

The Six Stages of Color

In the author's opinion, color expression in architecture has gone through five stages and is entering a sixth.

In the first era, Egypt, the Chaldees, India, China, color was symbolic and spoke the language of mysticism, religion and culture.

In the second era, Greece (and Rome to some extent), the traditions of the old school were formalized. Color was applied with a greater respect for form, composition, and contour, although the palette was not changed.

In the third era, Byzantine and early Gothic, color was decorative, used for the sake of its own intrinsic beauty, esthetically and not symbolically or formally.

In the fourth era, late Gothic, with the classic revival of the Renaissance and the influence of the Reformation, color was banished from the exterior of buildings and stripped of all symbolic or emotional purpose.

In the fifth and present era a certain ambivalence is to be noted. On the one hand are great buildings which reflect the gray starkness of the past, and on the other hand are buildings, usually commercial, in which color has been vividly applied. The two are strangers to each other, yet living in the same age and presumably catering to the same people.

If there is to be a new enfoldment, a sixth era, what will take place? The author ventures the hope that color and form will be one. The application of hue must be functional in that it must enhance design rather than distract from it or compete with it. Let there be symbolism, formality, decoration, but let color and form be united. Let the conception of hue go hand in hand with the conception of design and not come as an afterthought.

Surely the modern architect must turn his back on a gray age. Beauty in architecture has been lonely and incomplete without color. Color belongs with architecture. However, the designer must now create and not repeat. He must not have a mere "feeling" for color but a real knowledge of it. He must seize upon a strange but promising viewpoint made possible by a more thorough understanding of the spectrum and of the human and psychological nature of color as sensation. Through a sound application of principles unknown to other generations, he may attain a supremacy that will make the best efforts of his predecessors fade into historic obscurity.

16

The Nature
of Light

The study of color in architecture, design, and decoration belongs properly in the realm of art and psychology, not physics. Yet it is a curious fact that most books on the general subject of color devote extensive space to the mechanistic nature of light. This conceivably is useful to those interested in color measurement and in the intricacies of atoms and electromagnetic waves, but it hardly applies to beauty, to the physiological and psychological responses of human beings. As Arthur Eddington has written, "Whenever we state the properties of a body [or of radiant energy] in terms of physical quantities we are imparting knowledge as to the response of various metrical indications to its presence, *and nothing more* . . . There is a doctrine known to philosophers that the moon ceases to exist when no one is looking at it."

Obviously color needs the human approach. To continue with Eddington: "A rainbow described in the symbolism of physics is a band of aethereal vibrations arranged in systematic order of wave length from about .000040 cm. to .000072 cm. From one point of view we are paltering with the truth whenever we admire the gorgeous bow of color, and should strive to reduce our minds to such a state that we receive the same impressions from the rainbow as from a table of wave lengths. But although that is how the rainbow impresses itself on an impersonal spectroscope, we are not giving the whole truth and significance of experience — the starting point of the problem — if we suppress the factors wherein we ourselves differ from a spectroscope. We cannot say that the rainbow, as part of the world, was meant to convey the vivid effects of color; but we can perhaps say that the human mind as part of the world was meant to perceive it that way."

Electromagnetic Energy

However, a few notes on the physics of light may be in order. A satisfactory answer to the phenomenon of electromagnetic energy is still to come. With the discoveries of Newton and Hooke, light has at times been described in terms of particles whirling through space and in terms of waves. A plausible explanation is, perhaps, to be found in both.

According to the conclusions of such scientists as Planck, Bohr, and Einstein, radiant energy (visible light and color) is said to be propagated through space in the form of electromagnetic energy. A substance excited to luminosity by heat or electricity radiates certain waves, depending on its composition. This collection of waves is characteristic of the substance and may be analyzed in a spectroscope. Further, the waves that a substance will emit when excited will be identical with those it will absorb when radiant energy falls upon it.

Such energy, however, has a corpuscular structure as well. This means that it has tangible substance, that it actually "pushes," and that its mass may be bent by the force of gravity. The sun emits rays, the material pressure of which is said to equal about 250 tons a minute. Anyone who has seen a radiometer in the window of an optical supply store will have noted

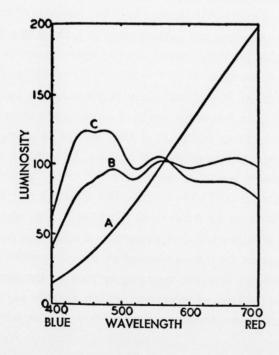

The spectral distribution of tungsten incandescent light (A), average noon sunlight (B), and north sky light (C).

the spinning of tiny squares supported on the point of a needle. These squares are black on one side and silver on the other and turn about under the action of light. The black surfaces absorb the light, react to the energy and thereupon are pushed, whereas the silver surfaces cause the light to be cast aside through reflection.

The Electromagnetic Spectrum

The complete spectrum of electromagnetic energy is charted in an arbitrary arrangement of sixty or seventy "octaves." It begins at one end with radio waves of exceedingly great wave length, proceeds through infrared rays, visible light, ultraviolet, and reaches its other extreme in the infinitesimally short waves of x-rays, gamma rays, and cosmic rays.

All this energy travels at the same rate of speed — about 186,000 miles a second — but differs in length of waves as measured from crest to crest. Though mathematics of a rather fabulous order may be involved, measurements of the speed of light, of frequencies and wave lengths, are extremely accurate and are generally accepted throughout the scientific world.

Divisions of the Electromagnetic Spectrum

Radio rays. These are the longest rays of all and may measure several thousand feet from crest to crest. They are employed in "wireless," ship-to-shore communication, and the like.

Induction heat. Long radio waves are used to raise the temperature of metals for hardening.

Commercial broadcasting. These waves "bounce" back from the ionosphere of the sky and will travel completely around the earth.

Short-wave broadcasting. This "octave" is used for police, ship, and amateur broadcasting. Part of the energy is employed in diathermy to generate heat in the body for the relief of rheumatism, arthritis, and neuralgia.

Next follow FM radio, television, and radar, the waves getting shorter and ranging from several meters to a fraction of a meter. The energy, however, penetrates the ionosphere and is not reflected back. Because the energy follows a straight path, rebroadcasting points are required for long distance transmission.

Infrared rays. Here is the energy that will penetrate heavy atmosphere. In the form of radiant heat it is emitted by infrared lamps, electric heaters, and steam radiators.

Visible light. Only a very small fraction of electromagnetic energy is seen by the eye. Visible light rays measure about 1/33,000 of an inch at the red end to about 1/67,000 of an inch at the violet end. While the human eye is insensitive to adjacent energy, insects may be blind to red waves but may respond to the stimulation of ultraviolet and x-rays.

Ultraviolet rays. These cause fluorescence, produce sun tan, account for the synthetic production of vitamin D, and have bactericidal properties.

X-rays. Soft x-rays (Grenz rays) are used for certain superficial skin diseases. Higher voltages and shorter frequencies — as short as 1/2,500,000 of an inch — are employed for diagnostic purposes, deep-seated afflictions, and the detection of flaws in metal.

Gamma rays. Next follow the radium rays discovered by Pierre and Marie Curie which are used to cure many forms of cancer. Here also are the emanations from nuclear fission associated with the atom bomb and the bombardment of the atom nucleus.

Cosmic rays. These are the shortest of all. Still a mystery, they probably are produced beyond the earth's atmosphere and spread their energy throughout the universe.

Diagram of the complete electromagnetic spectrum showing relative order of different types of radiation. All this energy travels at the same rate of speed, about 186,000 miles a second.

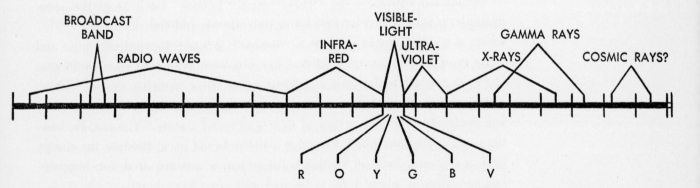

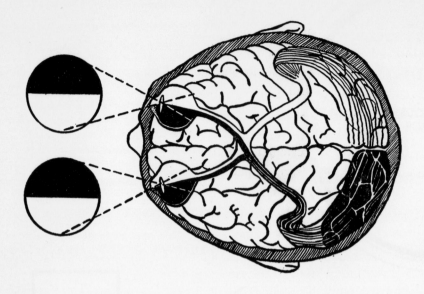

Color Vision

How the eye sees color is a mystery. "What happens when light acts upon a photoreceptor is essentially unknown" (Legrand H. Hardy). Some theories of color vision are mechanical, some electrical, some chemical. Confusion exists, not so much in understanding the optics of seeing, as in what takes place on the retina and in the brain.

The optical system of the eye is none too perfect. The lens system, for example, is such that color and forms may appear blurred. Yet if the mechanism is wanting, the brain does a remarkable job of compensation.

As most people know, the human eye functions somewhat like a camera. Over the eyeball is the cornea, a transparent outer covering shaped like a watch crystal. Behind this is the iris, a ringlike structure which expands and contracts under the action of light and which forms the pupil. Behind the pupil is the lens which bulges or flattens out to accommodate for closeness or distance. Back of all this is the retina, a network of sensitive nerve endings. Here is where light is focused and from here impulses are transmitted to the brain.

Human vision is characterized by an ability to see well under widely different conditions of illumination. If man cannot see at night as well as

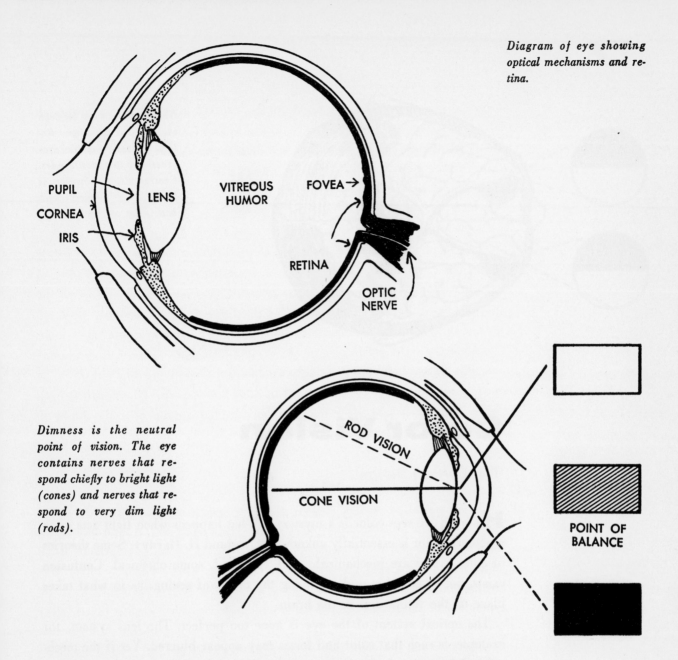

Diagram of eye showing
optical mechanisms and retina.

PUPIL

CORNEA

IRIS

LENS

VITREOUS
HUMOR

FOVEA →

RETINA

OPTIC
NERVE

*Dimness is the neutral
point of vision. The eye
contains nerves that re-
spond chiefly to bright light
(cones) and nerves that respond to very dim light
(rods).*

ROD VISION

CONE VISION

POINT OF
BALANCE

an owl or cat, his daylight vision is superior. If he cannot tolerate full sunlight like an eagle or a prairie dog, he does not have to retire when the sun
goes down. His is the best of all eyesight for the widest possible variety
of needs.

The Photoreceptors of the Eye

"Structurally, the retina may be regarded as a light-sensitive expansion
of the brain" (W. D. Wright). In the human retina there are two types
of photoreceptor cells: the rods (about 130,000,000 in each eye), distributed
rather uniformly over the entire expanse, and the cones (about 7,000,000),

especially numerous and refined in the central area or fovea. Although much is still to be learned, low intensity twilight vision is thought to be a function of the rods of the retina and high intensity daylight vision a function of the cones. The rods therefore react chiefly to brightness and motion in subdued light. The cones, quite numerous in the very center of the eye, react to brightness and motion and also see color. Thus most of the process of seeing takes place in the central or foveal area of the eye.

The fovea is permeated by a yellowish pigment. Although it measures less than 1/16 inch in diameter, it is crowded with tens of thousands of photoreceptors, each of which is believed to have its own connection to the brain. Hence there is good reason for the fovea to be remarkably sensitive to fine detail. In the periphery or outer boundaries of the retina, nerve connections are arranged in groups. As Wright observes, "This in turn implies that the peripheral retina is quite incapable of resolving fine detail in an image, although at the same time it enables the response from weak stimuli to be summated and gives the periphery an advantage over the fovea in the detection of faint images."

The Cortical Retina

In the so-called cortical region of the human brain there are areas connected with the fovea and periphery of the retina. However, it is an interesting fact that although the area devoted to peripheral vision is relatively small that devoted to foveal vision is relatively large. This means, in effect, that while the fovea is little more than a dot on the retina, its function in responding to detail and color is quite vital and requires a sizable bit of "gray matter."

The fact that the right side of the brain controls the left side of the body (and the converse) applies also in a rather strange way to vision. The corresponding halves of both retinas connect with their own side of the brain. Thus the right half of the right retina and the right half of the left retina, which together see the left side of the world, send their fibers to the right side of the brain. Some authorities, however, believe that the foveal cones connect with both sides of the brain.

Obviously, vision is as much in the brain as it is in the eye. Men see better than lower animals because they have superior brains. As Southall writes, "Good and reliable eyesight is a faculty that is acquired only by a long process of training, practice, and experience. Adult vision is the result of an accumulation of observations and associations of ideas of all sorts and is

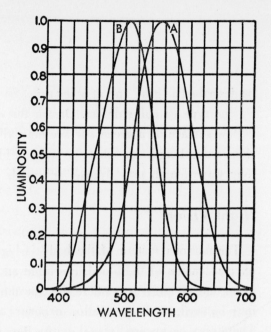

Brightness curves for daylight and twilight vision. In full light (A) the point of highest visibility is yellow. In very dim light (B) the point of highest visibility is blue-green.

therefore quite different from the untutored vision of an infant who has not yet learned to focus and adjust his eyes and to interpret correctly what he sees. Much of our young lives is unconsciously spent in obtaining and coordinating a vast amount of data about our environment, and each of us has to learn to use his eyes to see just as he has to learn to use his legs to walk and his tongue to talk."

Color Blindness

Color blindness may be congenital or it may, in rare cases, be acquired. When a person is born color-blind, there is usually no loss in the ability to have good vision for brightness, form, and detail. The defect is transmitted mainly through the distaff side of the family, the frequency among men being as high as 10 per cent and among women less than $\frac{1}{2}$ per cent.

Acquired color blindness may occur in diseases of the eye, optic tract, or cortex. It may accompany anemia, vitamin B deficiency, exposure to certain poisons such as carbon disulfide, lead, or thallium. Total color blindness and acquired color blindness almost always involve a general deficiency of vision. Hence a study of them is seldom of much value to an understanding of what healthy persons see.

Normally a person sees in terms of light-dark, yellow-blue and red-green. Where there is disturbance or deficiency, there may be abnormal green function or red function.

Most common is a good discrimination of yellow-blue but not of red-green (dichromatism). The majority of color-blind individuals fall into this classification. To quote Wright, "For instance, a gray surface may sometimes be described as gray and at other times be referred to as blue-green or purple by one type of color defect. Or, on the other hand, a red surface, a dark yellow surface or a green surface may all be described as brown." Hues of short wave length are likely to appear bluish (not greenish), and lines of long wave length may appear yellowish (not red or orange).

Night Vision

The nervous system of the body is highly sensitive to a lowering of the oxygen tension of the blood. So-called anoxia (oxygen shortage) may occur at normal air pressures where the concentration of oxygen in the atmosphere may be weak, or it may follow exposure to the "thin" air of high altitudes. There may be lowered visual acuity, less sensitivity to brightness and color, and partial or complete disappearance of afterimages. Voluntary eye movements may be disturbed, and tasks such as reading made difficult. In dive bombing, temporary loss of vision may take place under high speeds and high pressure. However, if suction is maintained over the eyeball, "blackout" may be prevented.

As illumination grows dim, the color-sensitive cones of the eye grow dormant and the process of seeing is taken over by the color-blind rods. The first colors to fade out are red. In soft twilight or starlight, all colors will be grayish.

An interesting experiment may be performed on sleepless nights to check the difference between cone vision and rod vision. After being in the dark for half an hour or more, cup the palm of the hand over one eye and expose the other eye to a lighted lamp. In darkness again, vision will be quite acute in the dark-adapted eye and quite blind in the eye that has been exposed to light. Again, with a selection of colored yarns or a color chart, the dark-adapted eye (in dim light) will be quite unable to detect hue difference. Yet the light-adapted eye (with the light on) will have excellent discrimination.

Negroes are said to see better in dim light than persons of other races. Brown-eyed persons may have lower thresholds than persons with blue eyes. Vitamin A deficiency and, indeed, poor diet will lessen the ability of the eye to see at night.

World War II led to a knowledge of the fact that dark-adaption may be accelerated. Ordinarily at least thirty minutes are required for the rods of the eye to gain full sensitivity. However, moderate stimulation of taste, cold, and physical effort may reduce the period and enable the eye to achieve dark-adaptation in a shorter time.

Color

Organization

Any number of color charts and color solids have been devised over the years. Newton arranged the first of all color circles in the latter part of the seventeenth century, choosing red, orange, yellow, green, blue, indigo, and violet as his chief hues and allying them to the proverbial seven planets and the seven notes of the diatonic music scale.

A generation later (1730) a German engineer by the name of Le Blond discovered the primary nature of red, yellow and blue in the mixture of pigments, his work being independently confirmed by Gautier of Paris. A century later Sir David Brewster worked out the now familiar red-yellow-blue concept later championed by Goethe, Schopenhauer, and Chevreul.

In color solids, R. Waller in 1689 designed a rectangular chessboard, placing blues and greens along one edge and reds and yellows along the other. Areas between portrayed intermediate mixtures. In 1745 Tobias Mayer used a red, yellow, blue triangle. Secondary hues ran along the sides and tertiaries toward the center. Further triangles showed white mixtures and black mixtures.

Lambert's pyramid (1772) was the first color solid to have appreciable merit. He also chose triangles having red, yellow, and blue primaries. Subsequent triangles included admixtures with white, these triangles growing increasingly smaller as they approached a white apex.

Runge in 1810 designed a color sphere, Ogden Rood of America a double cone: "In this double cone, then, we are at last able to include all the colors which under any circumstances we are able to perceive."

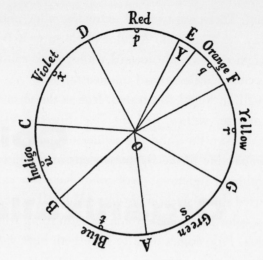

Newton's organization of color, the first of all known color circles.

Three Aspects of Color

Color organization may be approached from three different viewpoints, and each has its own merit. In *light rays* the physicist is able to settle upon red, green, and blue-violet. Red and green light will form yellow; green and blue-violet will form turquoise blue; red and blue-violet will form magenta red. All three combined will form white.

These same secondaries, yellow, turquoise blue, and magenta red, become primaries of average *colorants* such as ordinary pigments and dyes. In fact, red, green, and blue-violet filters are employed by the engraver to produce the blue, red, and yellow plates for process printing.

In *vision*, however, the psychologist has well established the primitive nature of four colors, red, yellow, green, and blue. Visual mixtures of yellow and blue on a color-wheel, for example, do not form green but gray. Red and green do not form yellow but a dull brown. To all indications the eye sees red, yellow, green, and blue as individual and unique sensations which bear no resemblance to each other. Psychologically, orange may look like red and like yellow, but neither red nor yellow look like orange.

Color organization today, however, is concerned almost wholly with an orderly cross section of the world of vision and not specifically with light or pigment mixtures. This organization has a very simple basis and is followed more or less by all theorists.

Color is three-dimensional. There are two end extremes, white and black, connected by a vertical gray scale or axis. A color circle or belt is placed midway about this axis. Light colors scale toward white; dark colors scale toward black; and grayish colors scale toward the neutral axis.

One set of color terms will be found illustrated. *Hue* is the term used to signify pure colors, red, orange, yellow, and the like. Spectral variations are hue differences. Up and down the solid are *values* or degrees of lightness which are directly comparable to the lightness steps of the gray scale. Whitish colors have high value or lightness; dark colors have low value. On a horizontal plane are charted differences in *chroma* (Munsell), *saturation*, or *intensity*. Vermilion is a color of strong chroma or saturation, while rose has weak or medium chroma. Pale colors usually have both high value and weak chroma.

The ISCC-NBS Method

Some years ago the Inter-Society Color Council in collaboration with the National Bureau of Standards worked out a simple method of describing colors with words. Based on the color solid mentioned above and allied to

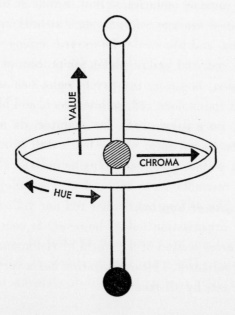

The three commonly recognized dimensions of color. Hues run in a circle about a neutral gray axis. Values run in vertical scales from light to dark. Chromas (intensity or saturation) run in horizontal scales from pure color to gray.

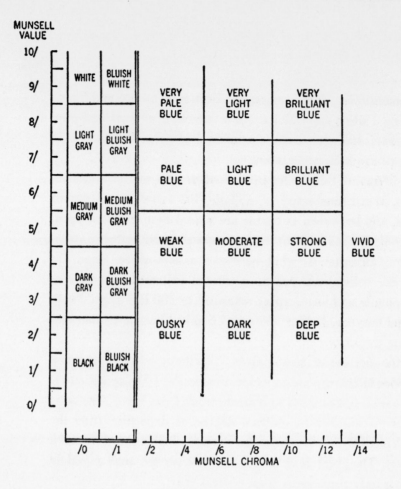

MUNSELL CHROMA

The Inter-Society Color Council-National Bureau of Standards method of color designation with words. The system is coordinated with Munsell.

the Munsell System, the world of color was charted and a limited number of terms chosen to coordinate the whole idea. All but very grayish colors are described by hue names (red, yellow, green, blue, purple, etc.) preceded by modifiers such as pale, bright, brilliant; weak, moderate, strong, vivid; dusky, dark, deep. For very grayish colors, hue names become modifiers of white, gray or black (bluish white, bluish gray, bluish black, etc.).

The purpose has been to try to reduce color description to a sensible and understandable basis. The system has been applied on various occasions and is used, for example, in color descriptions of drugs and chemicals in the U. S. Pharmacopoeia. After some years of experience, the general terminology is at present being strengthened and improved.

The Munsell System

Today there are two major systems of color that may lay claim to wide recognition. These are the creations of Albert H. Munsell and Wilhelm Ostwald. Both systems have certain elements in common. Both plot the entire realm of visual sensation in orderly sequence; both hold to a three-dimensional concept having a white and black apex, a vertical gray axis, and pure hues about an equator; and both include a method of color designation in which measured steps are accurately noted.

The color solid of Munsell follows the general shape of a sphere. However, because pure colors do not have equal value, hues such as yellow are placed near the white apex, and hues such as purple are placed near the black apex. Again, colors of strong chroma or saturation, such as pure red, extend farther from the neutral gray axis than do weak hues such as blue-green. There are ten major hues (red, yellow-red, yellow, green-yellow, green, blue-green, blue, purple-blue, purple and red-purple) arranged in 100 hue steps. There are nine value steps between perfect white and black. Chroma or intensity steps vary according to purity.

In designation, the element of hue is given a symbolic letter (sometimes preceded by a number to correspond to its location on the 100-step equator). The second identification is a number to indicate value from 1 to 9. The third identification is also a number to indicate degree of departure from the neutral gray axis. Thus PB 7/6 is a lavender having a high value (7) and a medium chroma (6). The color R 5/3 is a soft grayish red with a middle value of 5 and being only three steps from neutral gray.

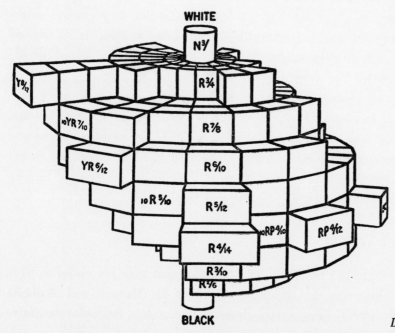

Diagram of the Munsell Color Solid.

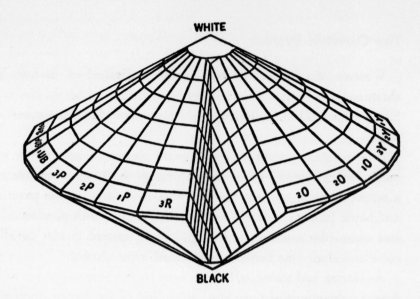

WHITE

BLACK

Diagram of the Ostwald Color Solid.

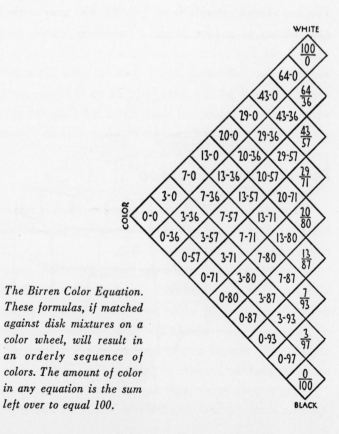

Section of the Ostwald Color Solid:

				a
			ca	c
		ea	ec	
	ga	gc	e	
ia	ic	ge		
la	lc	ie	g	
na	nc	ig		
pa	ne	lg	i	
pc	ng	li		
pe	ni	l		
pg	nl			
pi	n			
pl				
pn				
p				

Section of the Ostwald Color Solid. Gray scale is at right, with a standing for white and p for black. First letters indicate white content as on the gray scale; second letters indicate black content.

WHITE

COLOR

BLACK

The Birren Color Equation. These formulas, if matched against disk mixtures on a color wheel, will result in an orderly sequence of colors. The amount of color in any equation is the sum left over to equal 100.

The Ostwald System

Whereas the Munsell system finds its dimensions in hue, value, and chroma, Ostwald is concerned with hue, white, and black. His solid has the form of a double cone. There are 24 hues about the equator and eight value steps.

In the author's opinion the Ostwald system is beautifully and ideally related to the psychology of vision. Each of the 24 hues is made to comprise a monochromatic triangle having 28 tones. Vertical scales parallel to white and black (the isochromes) have equal purity. Scales parallel to pure color and white (the isotones) have equal black content. Scales parallel to pure color and black (the isotints) have equal white content.

As Hering had stated, all colors seen by the human eye are to be derived from combinations of pure hue, white, and black. Every sensation is a psychological unity of these three elements. Pleasing color sequence and color harmony, therefore, find "natural laws" in the organization of Ostwald's solid — a fact well verified by practical observation.

In his notations, Ostwald uses a simple combination of numbers and letters. The hue circuit extends from 1 to 24. The gray scale is given letters from *a* (for white) to *p* (for black). Two such letters, however, are always employed, the first letter indicating *white* content as on the gray scale and the second letter indicating *black* content. (See illustration of the Ostwald triangle.) Thus 7 *pa* is a pure red; 22 *ea* is a pale green with an *e* amount of white and an *a* amount of black as traced from the gray scale; 14 *li* is a deep grayish blue with an *l* amount of white and an *i* amount of black.

The Birren Color Equation

The work of Ostwald has inspired a similar approach to color order by the author which led (1934) to a mathematical interpretation of the Hering color-white-black principle.

If the reader will study the Color Equation, its order and organization will be readily understood. A right-angle triangle is given three terminal points in pure color, white and black. All formulas refer to proportions of mixture on a color-wheel. The first number in each instance refers to white content; the second number refers to black content; the sum of these two numbers plus the amount of color in the mixture always totals 100!

Using a pure color such as red, for example, if all the 45 equations are spun on a color-wheel and the results matched in pigments or paints, a beau-

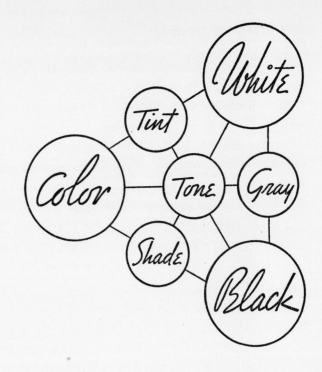

tiful series of color sequences will result which blend neatly and harmoniously in all directions — vertically, horizontally, obliquely toward white or obliquely toward black. Here are a few added points to be noted.

The gray scale runs vertically at the right, all formulas totalling 100. This scale, incidentally, is logarithmic in design, for a mid-gray in a color-wheel mixture of black and white will require a proportion of about 20 per cent white and 80 per cent black.

Scales having uniform proportions of white run parallel to pure color and black. Here the pale tone is strong and light, and the deep tone grayish and dark.

Scales having uniform proportions of black run parallel to pure color and white. In each row the pale tone is weak and dark, and the deep tone grayish and light.

Scales running parallel to the gray scale have hue content which is apparently uniform to the eye. Here each vertical row has exceptional beauty. Ostwald called such colors the shadow series. They comprise a relatively new sequence of beauty which unfortunately has been neglected in most formal systems of color harmony.

A Simplified Concept

Refer now to the Color Triangle and consider its simple features as a psychological interpretation of the world of color and how the human eye sees it. There are three primary color forms, so to speak, pure color (any and all, red, yellow, green, blue, etc.), white, and black. Each of these is distinct and unique in sensation.

When these three primaries are combined they produce four secondary forms, gray, tint, shade, tone. White and black produce gray. Pure hue and white produce tints which are whitish in quality. Pure hue and black produce shades which are blackish in quality. A combination of all three primaries, pure color, white *and* black, produces tones which are grayish in quality. The secondary forms resemble their primary components. That is, tints have both a white and a hue quality; shades have both a black and a hue quality; tones show traces of all three primary forms.

Realize that all colors seen by the human eye will classify as one of these seven forms! Despite infinite frequencies and variations, the eye (and the brain) tend to reduce all sensation to a simple order.

Appendix

AMERICAN COLORIST: Designed by Faber Birren. Booklet of charts contains over 500 color samples in process printing. Widely used in the field of horticulture and floral arrangement for color identification and contest judging. Available at $1.00 from the American Crayon Company, Sandusky, Ohio.

ARTISTS' OIL PAINTS: Minimum standards to assure satisfactory color, working qualities and permanence in oil paints used by artists. Adopted by a conference of manufacturers, distributors and users. Commercial Standard, CS98-42, U. S. Department of Commerce, National Bureau of Standards. Available from U. S. Government Printing Office, Washington, D. C.

AVIATION OBSTRUCTION MARKING: Regulations and Standards published by the U. S. Department of Commerce, Civil Aeronautics Administration, Washington, D. C. Describes required use of International Orange and White for the marking of obstructions near aircraft landing areas.

BATHROOM ACCESSORIES: A group of 7 colors for bathroom accessories: white, bath green, orchid, ivory, maize, bath blue, royal blue. Accepted by the National Retail Dry Goods Association and approved by a conference of manufacturers, distributors and users. (Colors are now largely obsolete.) Commercial Standard, CS63-38, U. S. Department of Commerce, National Bureau of Standards. Available from U. S. Government Printing Office, Washington, D. C.

BRITISH COLOUR COUNCIL: This agency issues seasonal color cards for women's, men's, and children's fashions. It also serves British industry in numerous ways, setting up standards for various purposes. Address, 13 Portman Square, London, W. 1, England.

BRITISH COLOUR COUNCIL DICTIONARY OF COLOUR STANDARDS (Second Edition): One of the most important English publications and very useful in America. Contains 240 samples of actual textiles, with a separate and valuable index of color names. Widely used as a standard reference on textiles and consumer goods. Available at $27.00 from British Colour Council, 13 Portman Square, London, W. 1, England.

BRITISH COLOUR COUNCIL DICTIONARY OF COLOURS FOR INTERIOR DECORATION: One of the most impressive publications on color ever issued. Contains 378 color samples in gloss, matte and pile fabric, with an important and convenient index of color names. Used for color identification and coordination. Two large volumes boxed with separate index. Available at $75.00 from British Colour Council, 13 Portman Square, London, W. 1, England.

BRITISH STANDARDS INSTITUTE: An English standardizing agency. Uniform practices and standards have been issued for ready-mixed paints; vitreous enamel finishes; light signals; identification of chemical pipe lines; engine room piping; pipes, conduits and cables in buildings; gas cylinders; medical gas cylinders; flat finish wall paints, process printing inks; camouflage paints; foundry patterns; etc. Address,

24/28 Victoria Street, Westminster, London, S. W. 1, England.

BRITISH TRADITIONAL COLOURS: Contains historical review of British traditions in color, heraldry, etc. Standard samples are shown of the colors of the Union Flag, the ribbons of noble orders of Knighthood, bunting colors of the British Navy, Army and Air Force, Heraldic colors, and authoritative Tartan colors. Issued by the British Colour Council, 13 Portman Square, London, W. 1, England.

BULLETIN COLORS: Standards in paints for posters, sign boards, etc. are recognized by the Outdoor Advertising Association, and are available from a number of paint companies.

CAMOUFLAGE COLORS: Three sets of standards have been issued by the Government. Specification T-1213, Supplement A and B, includes nine colors used by the U. S. Army, Corps of Engineers, Washington, D. C. A series of 16 Navy standards is available through U. S. Navy, Bureau of Yards and Docks, Washington, D. C. A series of 19 Army-Navy Aircraft Camouflage Standards issued by the Supply Officer, U. S. Naval Aircraft Factory, Philadelphia, Pa.

CARPET AND RUG COLOR CARD: Contains 21 carpeting samples for purposes of decoration and to include well known colors of more or less stable popularity. Price $12.50. Issued in cooperation with the Carpet Institute by The Color Association of the U. S., 200 Madison Avenue, New York, N. Y.

CAST STONE: A group of 14 colors for the finish of cast stone. Recommended

Commercial Standard, CS53-35, U. S. Department of Commerce, National Bureau of Standards. Available from U. S. Government Printing Office, Washington, D. C.

CHESKIN COLOR SYSTEM: Contains 48 charts having a total of 4,800 colors all derived from mixtures of three basic pigments with white and black. Prepared for use by designers, architects, decorators and others interested in color. Published at $75.00 by Color Research Institute of America, 176 West Adams Street, Chicago, Ill.

CHROMATIC REFLECTANCE STANDARDS: A series of porcelain-enamel panels having a high degree of permanence and used for purposes of comparison, color measurement and the calibration of photometers and colorimeters. Issued by the National Bureau of Standards, Washington, D. C.

COLOR-AID: A collection of 200 colors in book or sheet form. Of value where a good assortment of hues is wanted. Issued by Color-Aid Co., 329 E. 29th Street, New York, N. Y.

COLOR APTITUDE TEST: Prepared by a committee of the Inter-Society Color Council. A fairly difficult and therefore useful test to evaluate human ability to see small differences in color. May be used to screen workers who must have accurate color judgment. Available at $125.00 from Federation of Paint and Varnish Production Clubs, 121 South Broad Street, Philadelphia.

COLOR ASSOCIATION OF THE U. S.: One of the foremost standardizing and styling agencies in America. Seasonal color cards are issued for woolens, manmade fabrics and silks, women's gloves, and women's hosiery. (See Standard Color Card of America.) Headquarters for many color standards and for special service to members. Address, 200 Madison Avenue, New York, N. Y.

COLOR HARMONY MANUAL (Third Edition): A new presentation of the Ostwald System in 37 loose leaf charts and 943 individual acetate color chips having dull and glossy surfaces on op-

posite sides. One of the most beautiful collections of color standards ever assembled. Widely used throughout America in industry, art and education. Accompanying text, and excellent booklet on color names. Price, $150.00. Issued by Color Standards Department, Container Corporation of America, 38 South Dearborn Street, Chicago, Ill.

COLOR HELM: An ingenious device for the study of color coordination, designed by Joseph P. Gaugler, Associate Director, American Color Trends. Available in charts of five different types. Large Professional Color Helm contains 80 standards and is priced at $25.00. Color Helm, Inc., Ridgewood, N. J.

COLOR MATERIALS FOR ART EDUCATION IN SCHOOLS: Recommended commercial standards for school art materials, chalks, crayons, water colors, etc. prepared by the Crayon, Water Color, and Craft Institute. Commercial Standard CS130-46, U. S. Department of Commerce National Bureau of Standards. Available from U. S. Government Printing Office, Washington, D. C.

COLOR TERMS: An excellent reference for color names will be found in The ISCC — NBS Method of Designating Colors and a Dictionary of Color Names, National Bureau of Standards Circular 553. Available from Superintendent of Documents, U. S. Government Printing Office, Washington, D. C., for $2.00.

COLORIZER SYSTEM: An excellent and complete color system containing over 1,000 standards impressively bound in a large volume. Offered by a cooperative group of American paint companies and available in most cities. Colorizer Associates, P. O. Box 1322, Salt Lake City, Utah.

COLOUR ATLAS: Contains 38 plates which exhibit 7,279 printed colors. There are 74 pages of text in Spanish and English and conversion tables of Ridgeway's standards. Proposed as a universal system of color specification. Designed by C. y J. Villalobos and published in Buenos Aires, Argentina.

COMPRESSED GAS CYLINDERS AND PIPELINES COLOR CODE: This military standard has been approved by Departments of the Army, Air Force, and Navy and is mandatory. Six colors are employed — yellow, brown, blue, green, gray, and red. MIL-STD-101 issued by Munitions Board Standard Agency and available from U. S. Government Printing Office, Washington, D. C.

CRAYONS, CHALKS, AND RELATED ART MATERIALS FOR SCHOOL USE: Standards designed to establish methods of testing, rating, certifying, and labeling. Simplified Practice Recommendation R-92-49, U. S. Department of Commerce, Washington, D. C.

DICTIONARY OF COLOR (Second Edition): Written by A. Maerz and M. Rea Paul. Shows over 7,000 samples, with color names based on historical origins and current usage. A valuable source for color reference, and one of the best lists of color names available. Published at $27.50 by McGraw-Hill Book Co., 330 West 42nd Street, New York, N. Y.

DRAPERY AND UPHOLSTERY FABRIC COLOR CARD: Contains 83 textile samples of popular colors having interest to manufacturers, retailers, decorators, and stylists. Issued in cooperation with the Decorative Fabrics Institute by The Color Association of the U. S., 200 Madison Avenue, New York, N. Y.

DU PONT CUSTOM COLORS: A well designed system of 572 colors derived from 30 base colorants. Available nationally to the paint industry through E. I. du Pont de Nemours & Co., Finishes Division, Wilmington, Del.

DUO-COLOR GUIDE: A well designed and complete showing of two-color engraving possibilities. Contains 100 pages and 4,200 different screen combinations of a color with black or a color with another color. Useful to engravers, printers, lithographers, commercial artists, etc. Published at $35.00 by Graphic Publishing Co., 270 Lafayette Street, New York, N. Y.

FACING TILE: Industry-wide color standards have been established in ceramic glaze, salt glaze, and natural clay structural facing tile. These comprise 24 colors chosen with the research assistance of Faber Birren & Company to simplify the problems of architects and to introduce certain principles of functionalism into building design. Issued through The Facing Tile Institute, 1520 18th Street, N. W., Washington, D. C.

× FEDERAL COLOR CARD: A Federal specification which standardizes the colors used throughout the Government. An important reference book for private industry as well. Contains 187 samples in gloss, semi-gloss, and lustreless finish in heavy binder. Prepared by General Services Administration and available from U. S. Government Printing Office, Washington, D. C.

FLAG OF THE UNITED STATES: Scientific definitions of the red, white, blue approved by all departments of the Government. Section IV, Federal Standards Stock Catalog. Specification TT-C-591, July 3, 1934, available from U. S. Government Printing Office, Washington, D. C. (Samples of the colors will be found in the Standard Color Card of America issued by The Color Association of the U. S.)

FOUNDRY PATTERNS ON WOOD: Standard system of making wood foundry patterns, using black, yellow, and red. Accepted by various associations. Commercial standard CS19-32, U. S. Department of Commerce, National Bureau of Standards. Available from U. S. Government Printing Office, Washington, D. C.

× FRENCH COLOR STANDARDS: Two widely used French sources for color standardization are: Code Universel des Couleurs by E. Seguy (720 samples), and special books published by The French Society of Crysanthemistes.

× GLENN COLORULE: An ingenious device to test the color vision of observers and the spectral quality of light sources. Also useful in illustrating the strange phenomenon of metamerism (colors that match under one light source but not under another). Available through

Sidney Blumenthal & Co., Rocky Mount, N. C.

GRAY FINISHES FOR INDUSTRIAL APPARATUS AND EQUIPMENT: Four standard gray finishes have been established in cooperation with various industries. Publication Z55.1-1950, American Standards Association, 70 E. 45th Street, New York, N. Y.

HIGHWAY SIGNS; STANDARD YELLOW: Issued by Public Roads Administration, Washington, D. C.

HORTICULTURAL COLOUR CHARTS: Two volumes, containing about 800 color samples. Used for color designation in horticulture and industry. Available from British Colour Council, 13 Portman Square, London, W. 1, England.

× INTER-SOCIETY COLOR COUNCIL: An effort to develop a standard designation for colors, using words commonly understood. Approved by various associations and applicable to widespread use in science, art, and industry. Research Paper RP1239, U. S. Department of Commerce, National Bureau of Standards, Washington, D. C. A new revision of the method is now in process.

KITCHEN ACCESSORIES: A group of 6 colors for kitchen accessories: white, kitchen green, ivory, delphinium blue, royal blue, red. Accepted by the National Retail Dry Goods Association and approved by a conference of manufacturers, distributors, and users. (Colors are now largely obsolete.) Commercial Standard, CS62-38, U. S. Department of Commerce. Available from U. S. Government Printing Office, Washington, D. C.

MANUAL ON UNIFORM TRAFFIC CONTROL DEVICES FOR STREETS AND HIGHWAYS: Prepared by a joint committee of American Association of State Highway Officials, Institute of Traffic Engineers, and National Conference on Street and Highway Safety. A.S.A. Standard D6.1-1948. Available from Public Roads Administration, Federal Works Agency, Washington, D. C.

MUNSELL BOOK OF COLOR: One of the

most widely accepted systems of color identification in the United States. The standards are broadly applied for color identification and description by American industry, science, and the U. S. Government. Contains over 900 samples. Large edition sells at $90.00 and pocket edition at $70.00. Available from Munsell Color Co., 10 East Franklin Street, Baltimore, Md.

× MUNSELL VALUE SCALES FOR JUDGING REFLECTANCE: Designed in collaboration with the Illuminating Engineering Society for illuminating engineers, architects, and interior decorators. Eleven charts show 179 swatches of color and give reflectances under tungsten light, daylight, and blue sky. Available at $15.00 from Munsell Color Co., 10 East Franklin Street, Baltimore, Md.

NATIONAL ELECTRICAL MANUFACTURERS ASSOCIATION: Standards have been established for the colors of flexible cords, glazed cotton braids, control cables, and Type SN building wire. (See Standard Color Card of America.)

× NU-HUE SYSTEM: This system involving about 1,000 colors derived from a line of basic paints, is one of the best yet devised. Standards are presented in the form of charts and individual cards. Formulas for the system have also been prepared to match the standards of the Color Harmony Manual. Issued by the Martin-Senour Company, 2520 South Quarry Street, Chicago, Ill.

PAINT PIGMENT STANDARDS FOR COLOR AND TINTING STRENGTH: Used to test paint pigments purchased in accordance with Federal specifications. Standard samples of 24 basic toners are available at $2.00 each from National Bureau of Standards, Washington, D. C.

PIPING IDENTIFICATION: Scheme for the uniform identification of piping systems in industry. Red for fire protection; yellow (or orange) for dangerous materials; green (white, black, or gray) for safe materials; blue for protective materials; purple for valuable materials. Publication A13-1928. Available from American Standards Association, 70 E. 45th Street, New York, N. Y.

PLASTICS: Two sets of industry-wide standards have been established to facilitate purchasing and production. A series of 18 colors for polystyrene plastics is described in Commercial Standard CS156-49. A series of 17 colors for molded urea plastics is described in Commercial Standard CS147-47. Both reports are available from the U. S. Government Printing Office, Washington, D. C. Actual samples of the plastics may be purchased at $2.50 per set from the Manufacturing Chemists Association, Woodward Building, 15th and H Streets, N. W., Washington, D. C.

PLOCHERE COLOR SYSTEM: One of the most complete color systems ever produced in America. Contains over 1,200 samples. A useful collection for anyone in need of a wide and well arranged assortment of colors. Available in two forms: 3x5 cards boxed at $55.00; book form with valuable index of color names at $50.00. G. Plochere, 1820 Hyperion Avenue, Los Angeles, Cal.

POISONS, EXPLOSIVES, GASES: The Interstate Commerce Commission recognizes and insists upon special labels for shipments of gases, inflammable liquids, explosives, acids, etc. The colors generally used are white, black, red, yellow, blue, green.

PROCESS COLORS: Adopted (1927) by the Standardization Committee of the American Institute of Graphic Arts and approved by the American Association of Advertising Agencies and the National Association of Advertisers. Recommended standards for process red, yellow, blue, black.

RADIO-TELEVISION MANUFACTURERS ASSOCIATION: Color standards have been established for Fixed Resistors. (See Standard Color Card of America.)

RIDGWAY, COLOR STANDARDS AND COLOR NOMENCLATURE: The most renowned historical work in America. Contains about 1,000 samples, each identified by name. Widely used by archaeologists and naturalists. Published by Robert Ridgway, Washington, D. C., 1912, but now out-of-print.

SAFETY COLOR CODE: Designed by Faber Birren in collaboration with du Pont. Contains 8 color standards used for purposes of safety and identification in industry. Code is widely employed by industry and is standard for U. S. Navy and Coast Guard. Description available from E. I. du Pont de Nemours & Co., Finishes Division, Wilmington, Del.

SAFETY COLOR CODE: A condensed version of the Faber Birren-du Pont Code (above) has been approved and revised in a second edition. Standard Z53.1-1953, American Standards Association, 70 E. 45th Street, New York, N. Y.

SANITARY WARE: Standard colors for plumbing fixtures and allied products made of vitreous china, enameled iron, etc. The colors are green, orchid, ivory, blue, light brown, black. Adopted by a conference of producers, distributors, and users. (Colors are now largely obsolete.) Commercial Standard, CS30-31, U. S. Department of Commerce, National Bureau of Standards. Available from U. S. Government Printing Office, Washington, D. C.

SCHOOL BUS CHROME: Standard yellow adopted for school buses and approved by representatives of the 48 State Departments of Education. Available from National Education Association, 1201 16th St., Washington, D. C.

SCHOOL FURNITURE: Standard colors for school furniture as adopted by a conference of producers, distributors, and buyers of school equipment. Simplified Practice Recommendation, R111-30, U. S. Department of Commerce, National Bureau of Standards. Available from U. S. Government Printing Office, Washington, D. C.

SEDIMENTARY ROCKS: Goldman and Merwin Color Chart, showing 115 colors for the description of sedimentary rocks. Available from Division of Geology and Geography, National Research Council, Washington, D. C.

SIGNAL GLASSES: Scientific description of colors used in signal glasses: red, yellow, green, blue, purple, lunar white. Signal Section Specification, 69-35, Association of American Railroads, Transportation Building, Washington, D. C.

SIGNS: A widely recognized code for the use of color in signs: red for danger; yellow for caution; green for safety instruction; blue for information, general notices, and slogans; black for direction signs. Publication Z35.1-1941. American Standards Association, 70 East 45th Street, New York, N. Y.

SMOKE; RINGELMANN'S SCALE FOR GRADING DENSITY: Four rectangular patterns to be viewed at a distance to determine density of smoke. Available from Publications Section, Bureau of Mines, U. S. Department of the Interior, Washington, D. C.

SOIL COLORS: A showing of 219 different colors of soil, intended for use by soil scientists, geologists, and archaeologists. Approved by Soil Survey Committee, U. S. Department of Agriculture. Available at $20.00 from Munsell Color Co., 10 East Franklin Street, Baltimore, Md.

SPECIFICATION AND DESCRIPTION OF COLOR: Widely used throughout American industry as a method of describing colors. Standard Z44-1942, issued by the American Standards Association, 70 E. 45th Street, New York, N. Y.

STANDARD COLOR CARD OF AMERICA: One of the most useful publications in America. Contains 216 samples of dyed silk in gloss and matte finish. Widely used for color identification and standardization, and an excellent source of reference for names. The colors incorporate U. S. Government standards for the Flag of the United States, service uniform colors, etc. They have also been adopted as standards by the National Bureau of Standards, National Electrical Manufacturers Association, Radio-Television Manufacturers Association, Manufacturing Chemists Association, and others. Published at $35.00 by

The Color Association of the U. S., 200 Madison Avenue, New York, N. Y.

⤬ STANDARD COLORS FOR BUSINESS PUBLICATIONS: A selection of five colors to be used as standard printing inks in business publications. Developed by American Association of Advertising Agencies, Associated Business Publications, and National Business Publications. Copies may be obtained from any one of these three organizations.

TRAFFIC CONTROL SIGNALS: Color standards have been set up for red, amber, and green lights used in traffic signals. Technical Report No. 1, ASA, D10.1-1942, American Standards Association, 70 E. 45th St., New York, N. Y.

U. S. ARMY, GENERAL PAINT SPECIFICATIONS: A showing of 72 colors in various finishes. Used by the Army in the purchase of paint and related materials. Supplement to No. 3-1, issued by the Quartermaster General, Washington, D. C. The Office of the Chief of Engineers, Department of the Army, Washington, D. C., also issues 9 color standards used for maintenance and repair, alterations, improvements, etc., in buildings owned or leased by the Army. Federal Specifications TT-P-47 and TT-P-40.

⤬ U. S. ARMY INK COLOR GUIDE: Shows 41 colors and 3 fluorescent inks used as a standard basis for the production of maps. Issued by Army Map Service, Corps of Engineers, U. S. Army, Washington, D. C.

U. S. ARMY RIBBONS FOR DECORATIONS AND SERVICE MEDALS: General color specifications for the ribbons used on medals and decorations. U. S. Army, Specification 7-3B, Quartermaster General, Washington, D. C.

U. S. ARMY STANDARD COLOR CARD: Army colors standardized for the different arms and services and approved by the Quartermaster General. Issued by Textile Color Card Association, 200 Madison Avenue, New York, N. Y. The Association also issues official color cards and standards for Slide Fastener Tapes and for Sewing Threads for Clothing and Equipage.

U. S. COAST GUARD, PAINT AND COLOR MANUAL: A comprehensive report covering all major facilities, including vessels and shore units. A series of 24 color standards is employed to promote simplification, maintenance, safety. Prepared with the assistance of Faber Birren & Company for the U. S. Coast Guard, Washington, D. C.

U. S. COLOR STANDARDS FOR PUBLIC BUILDINGS: Contains 117 standards. Colors are used as guides in the painting of Government buildings. Issued by Public Buildings Service, Washington, D. C.

U. S. NAVY, APPLICATION OF COLOR TO SHORE ESTABLISHMENT: A coordinated program designed to effect uniform practices in the use of color and paint. Covers shore facilities, industrial, administrative and personnel buildings, machinery and equipment, transportation equipment, etc. Includes a comprehensive safety code for color. Prepared by Faber Birren & Company for Bureau of Yards and Docks, U. S. Navy Department, Washington, D. C.

U. S. MARITIME COMMISSION STANDARD COLOR CARD: Contains 49 standards for topside and hull, ship interiors, striping enamels, deck paints, bottom paints, primers, etc. Also STANDARD COLORS FOR FLAGS. This publication contains standards for purchase of materials for flags, including International Code Flags. Available from U. S. Maritime Commission, Washington, D. C.

U. S. POST OFFICE DEPARTMENT OLIVE GREEN AND CREAM: Colors used as guides in the painting of trucks, mail boxes, and other Post Office equipment. Issued by Post Office Department, Washington, D. C.

WOOD OFFICE FURNITURE: A scientifically devised Softone finish for wood office furniture has been developed with the assistance of Faber Birren & Company and offered by an industry-wide group of manufacturers. Designed to improve visibility and seeing conditions in offices. Industry-wide standards have also been set for walnut, mahogany, golden oak, school brown. Available through the Wood Office Furniture Institute, 730 11th Street, N. W., Washington 5, D. C.

VETERANS ADMINISTRATION MASTER PAINT COLOR GUIDE: Contains 39 samples, with instructions for use in painting exteriors and interiors. Issued by Veterans Administration Construction Service, Color Design Unit, Washington, D. C.

Bibliography

Abbott, Arthur G., *The Color of Life*, McGraw-Hill Book Co., New York, 1947.

Allen, Frank, and Schwartz, Manuel, "The Effect of Stimulation of the Senses of Vision, Hearing, Taste and Smell Upon the Sensibility of the Organs of Vision," *Journal of General Physiology*, September 20, 1940.

Allen, Grant, *The Colour Sense*, Trubner & Co., London, 1879.

Alschuler, Rose H., and Hattwick, La Berta Weiss, *Painting and Personality*, University of Chicago Press, Chicago, 1947.

Babbitt, Edwin D., *The Principles of Light and Color*, published by the author, East Orange, N. J., 1896.

Birren, Faber, "Color Coding System for Marking Hazards," *Architectural Forum*, December, 1948.

Birren, Faber, "Color Conditioning, Aid to Getting Work Done," *Dun's Review*, January, 1949.

Birren, Faber, "Color in the Plant," *Factory Management and Maintenance*, February, 1945.

Birren, Faber, "Color Is More than Beauty," *Modern Hospital*, January, 1952.

Birren, Faber, "Color for Production," *Architectural Forum*, July, 1942.

Birren, Faber, *Color Psychology and Color Therapy*, McGraw-Hill Book Co., New York, 1950.

Birren, Faber, "Color and Psychotherapy," *Modern Hospital*, August-September, 1946.

Birren, Faber, "The Dollar Value of Color," *Banking*, December 15, 1950.

Birren, Faber, "The Emotional Significance of Color Preference," *American Journal of Occupational Therapy*, March-April, 1952.

Birren, Faber, *Functional Color*, Crimson Press, New York, 1937.

Birren, Faber, "Functional Color in the Schoolroom," *Magazine of Art*, April, 1949.

Birren, Faber, "Functional Color and the Architect," *Journal of The American Institute of Architects*, June-July, 1949.

Birren, Faber, "Functional Color in Hospitals," *Architectural Record*, May, 1949.

Birren, Faber, "Functionalism with Color," *The Nation's Schools*, May, 1947.

Birren, Faber, "A Guide to the Use of Color in Painting the Plant," *Factory Management and Maintenance*, June, 1949.

Birren, Faber, "Light Control vs. Light Intensity," *Transactions, American Academy of Ophthalmology and Otolaryngology*, May-June, 1950.

Birren, Faber, *Monument to Color*, McFarlane, Warde, McFarlane, New York, 1938.

Birren, Faber, "On Understanding Color," *Illuminating Engineering*, July, 1948.

Birren, Faber, "The Ophthalmic Aspects of Illumination, Brightness and Color," *Transactions, American Academy of Ophthalmology and Otolaryngology*, May-June, 1948.

Birren, Faber, "An Organic Approach to Illumination and Color," *Transactions, American Academy of Ophthalmology and Otolaryngology*, January-February, 1952.

Birren, Faber, "Put Color to Work," *American School and University*, Vol. 24, 1952-3.

Birren, Faber, "Renovate with Color," *Home Furnishings*, May, 1946.

Birren, Faber, *Selling with Color*, McGraw-Hill Book Co., New York, 1945.

Birren, Faber, "The Specification of Illumination and Color in Industry," *Transactions, American Academy of Ophthalmology and Otolaryngology*, January-February, 1947.

Birren, Faber, *The Story of Color*, Crimson Press, Westport, Conn., 1941.

Bissonnette, T. H. "Experimental Modification of Breeding Cycle in Goats," *Physiological Zoology*, July, 1941.

Blum, Harold F., *Photodynamic Action and Diseases Caused by Light*, Reinhold Publishing Corp., New York, 1941.

Boring, Edwin G., *Sensation and Perception in the History of Experimental Psychology*, Appleton-Century-Crofts, New York, 1942.

Bossert, Helmuth, *An Encyclopedia of Color Decoration*, Ernst Wasmuth, Berlin, 1928.

Bragdon, Claude, *Architecture and Democracy*, Alfred A. Knopf, New York, 1926.

Bragg, Sir William, *The Universe of Light*, Macmillan Co., New York, 1934.

Budge, E. A. Wallis, *Amulets and Superstitions*, Oxford University Press, New York, 1930.

Burris-Meyer, Elizabeth, *Color and Design in the Decorative Arts*, Prentice-Hall, Inc., New York, 1935.

Burris-Meyer, Elizabeth, *Decorating Livable Homes*, Prentice-Hall, Inc., New York, 1947.

Burris-Meyer, Elizabeth, *Historical Color Guide*, William Helburn, Inc., New York, 1938.

Bustanoby, J. H., *Principles of Color and Color Mixing*, McGraw-Hill Book Co., New York, 1947.

Cheney, Sheldon, *The New World Architecture*, Tudor Publishing Co., New York, 1936.

Cheskin, Louis, *Colors — What They Can Do for You*, Liveright Publishing Corp., New York, 1947.

Chevreul, M. E., *The Principles of Harmony and Contrast of Colours*, Bell & Daldy, London, 1870.

Cockerell, C. R., *The Temples of Jupiter Panhellenius and Apollo Epicurius*, John Weale, London, 1860.

Crace, John D., *The Art of Colour Decoration*, B. T. Botsford, London, 1912.

Deutsch, Felix, "Psycho-Physical Reactions of the Vascular System to Influences of Light and to Impressions Gained Through Light," *Folia Clinica Orientalia*, Vol. I, Fasc. 3 and 4, 1937.

Duggar, Benjamin M. (Editor), *Biological Effects of Radiation*, McGraw-Hill Book Co., New York, 1936.

Eastlake, John, *Goethe's Theories of Colours*, John Murray, London, 1840.

Eddington, A. S., *The Nature of the Physical World*, Macmillan Co., New York, 1948.

Ellinger, Friedrich, *The Biologic Fundamentals of Radiation Therapy*, Elsevier Publishing Co., New York, 1941.

Evans, Ralph M., *An Introduction to Color*, John Wiley & Sons, New York, 1948.

Fergusson, James, *A History of Architecture in All Countries*, John Murray, London, 1893.

Ferree, C. E. and Rand, Gertrude, "Lighting and the Hygiene of the Eye," *Archives of Ophthalmology*, July, 1929.

Ferree, C. E. and Rand, Gertrude, "Lighting in Its Relation to the Eye," *Proceedings of the American Philosophical Society*, Vol. LVII, No. 5, 1918.

Gesell, Arnold, Ilg, Frances L., and Bullis, Glenna E., *Vision, Its Development in Infant and Child*, Paul B. Hoeber, Inc., New York, 1949.

Goldstein, Kurt, *The Organism*, American Book Co., New York, 1939.

Goldstein, Kurt, "Some Experimental Observations Concerning the Influence of Color on the Function of the Organism," *Occupational Therapy and Rehabilitation*, June, 1942.

Guilford, J. P., "The Affective Value of Color as a Function of Hue, Tint, and Chroma," *Journal of Experimental Psychology*, June, 1934.

Hall, Manly P., *An Encyclopedic Outline of Masonic, Hermetic, Quabbalistic and Rosicrucian Symbolic Philosophy*, H. S. Crocker Co., San Francisco, 1928.

Hardy, LeGrand H., and Rand, Gertrude, "Elementary Illumination for the Ophthalmologist," *Archives of Ophthalmology*, January, 1945.

Harmon, D. B., "Lighting and Child Development," *Illuminating Engineering*, April, 1945.

Harmon, D. B., "Lighting and the Eye," *Illuminating Engineering*, September, 1944.

Henderson, D. K., and Gillespie, R. D., *A Text-Book of Psychiatry*, Oxford University Press, London, 1948.

Jacobson, Egbert, *Basic Color*, Paul Theobald, Chicago, 1948.

Jaensch, E. R., *Eidetic Imagery*, Kegan Paul, Trench, Trubner & Co., London, 1930.

Jeans, Sir James, *The Mysterious Universe*, Macmillan Co., New York, 1932.

Johnston, Earl S., *Sun Rays and Plant Life*, 1936 Report of Smithsonian Institution, Washington.

Judd, Deane B., "Facts of Color Blindness," *Journal of the Optical Society of America*, June, 1943.

Judd, Deane B., *Color in Business, Science and Industry*, John Wiley & Sons, Inc., New York, 1952.

Kandinsky, Wassily, *The Art of Spiritual Harmony*, Houghton Mifflin Co., Boston, 1940.

Karwoski, Theodore F. and Odbert, Henry S., "Color Music," *Psychological Monographs*, Vol. 50, No. 2, 1938, Ohio State University, Columbus.

Katz, David, *The World of Color*, Kegan Paul, Trench, Trubner & Co., London, 1935.

Ketcham, Howard, *How to Use Color and Decorating Designs in the Home*, Greystone Press, New York, 1949.

Klein, Adrian Bernard, *Colour-Music, The Art of Light*, Crosby Lockwood & Son, London, 1930.

Klopfer, Bruno and Kelley, Douglas McGlashan, *The Rorschach Technique*, World Book Co., Yonkers, N. Y., 1946.

Koffka, Kurt, *Principles of Gestalt Psychology*, Harcourt, Brace & Co., New York, 1935.

Köhler, Wolfgang, *Gestalt Psychology*, Liveright Publishing Co., New York, 1947.

Kouwer, B. J., *Colors and Their Character*, Martinus Nÿhoff, The Hague, 1949.

Kravkov, S. V., "Color Vision and the Autonomic Nervous System," *Journal of the Optical Society of America*, June, 1942.

Kuhn, Hedwig S., *Eyes and Industry*, C. V. Mosby Co., St. Louis, 1950.

Le Corbusier, *Towards a New Architecture*, John Rodher, London, 1927.

Luckiesh, M., "Brightness Engineering," *Illuminating Engineering*, February, 1944.

Luckiesh, M., *Light, Vision and Seeing*, D. Van Nostrand Co., New York, 1944.

Luckiesh, M., *The Science of Seeing*, D. Van Nostrand Co., New York, 1937.

Lythgoe, R. J., "The Measurement of

Visual Acuity," Special Report Series No. 173, Industrial Research Board of the Medical Research Council, London, 1932.

Maier, N. R. F. and Schneirla, T. C., *Principles of Animal Psychology*, McGraw-Hill Book Co., New York, 1935.

Morgan, L. D., "There Is Something Wrong with Our Fluorescent Lighting Systems," *Illuminating Engineering*, May, 1945.

Mosse, Eric P., "Color Therapy," *Occupational Therapy and Rehabilitation*, February, 1942.

Munsell, Albert H., *A Color Notation*, Munsell Color Co., Baltimore, 1926.

National Industrial Conference Board Management Record, "The Use of Color in Industry," New York, May, 1947.

Ostwald, Wilhelm, *Colour Science*, Winsor & Newton, London, 1931.

Polyak, S. L., *The Retina*, University of Chicago Press, Chicago, 1941.

Pope, Arthur, *The Painter's Modes of Expression*, Harvard University Press, Cambridge, 1931.

Porter, L. C. and Prideaux, G. F., "War on Insect Invaders," *Magazine of Light*, April 25, 1942.

Phillips, Lisle March, *Form and Colour*, Charles Scribner's Sons, New York, 1915.

Rickers-Ovsiankina, Maria, "Some Theoretical Considerations Regarding the Rorschach Method," *Rorschach Research Exchange*, April, 1943.

Sargent, Walter, *The Enjoyment and Use of Color*, Charles Scribner's Sons, New York, 1923.

Science of Color, prepared by Committee on Colorimetry, Optical Society of America, Thomas Y. Crowell Co., New York, 1953.

Simonson, Ernst and Brozek, Josef, "Effects of Illumination Level on Visual Performance and Fatigue," *Journal of the Optical Society of America*, April, 1948.

Sloan, Raymond P., *Hospital Color and Decoration*, Physicians' Record Co., Chicago, 1944.

Solon, Leon V., *Polychromy*, Architectural Record, New York, 1924.

Southall, James P. C., *Introduction to Physiological Optics*, Oxford University Press, New York, 1937.

Strecker, Edward A., Ebaugh, Franklin G., and Ewalt, Jack R., *Practical Clinical Psychiatry*, Blakiston Co., Philadelphia, 1948.

Sullivan, Louis H., *The Autobiography of an Idea*, Press of the American Institute of Architects, New York, 1924.

Tassman, I. S., *The Eye Manifestations of Internal Disease*, C. V. Mosby Co., St. Louis, 1946.

Thomson, J. Arthur, *The Outline of Science*, G. P. Putnam's Sons, New York, 1937.

Vinci, Leonardo da, *A Treatise on Painting*, George Bell & Sons, London, 1877.

Walls, G. L., *The Vertebrate Eye*, Cranbrook Press, Bloomfield Hills, Mich., 1942.

Ward, James, *Colour Decoration of Architecture*, Chapman and Hall, London, 1913.

Werner, Heinz, *Comparative Psychology of Mental Development*, Follett Publishing Co., Chicago, 1948.

Weston, H. C., "Proposals for a New Lighting Code," *Illuminating Engineering*, February, 1943.

Whitaker, Charles Harris, *The Story of Architecture*, Halcyon House, New York, 1934.

William, C. A. S., *Outlines of Chinese Symbolism*, Customs College Press, Peiping, China, 1931.

Wilson, Robert F., *Colour and Light at Work*, Seven Oaks Press, London, 1953.

Woolley, C. Leonard, *Ur of the Chaldees*, Charles Scribner's Sons, New York, 1930.

Wright, Frank Lloyd, *An Autobiography*, Longmans, Green & Co., New York, 1938.

Wright, W. D., *The Measurement of Colour*, Adam Hilger, Ltd., London, 1944.

Wright, W. D., *Researches on Normal and Defective Colour Vision*, C. V. Mosby Co., St. Louis, 1947.

Index

Index (continued)